NORTH BRITISH LOCOMOTIVE

A CATALOGUE OF NARROW GAUGE LOCOMOTIVES

NORTH BRITISH LOCOMOTIVE

A CATALOGUE OF NARROW GAUGE LOCOMOTIVES

A Reproduction of the
NORTH BRITISH LOCOMOTIVE COMPANY'S
CATALOGUE OF NARROW GAUGE LOCOMOTIVES
1912

Introduced by John Thomas with additional notes compiled by Alan Dunbar

DAVID & CHARLES REPRINTS

7153 4899 X

This Catalogue was originally published by
THE NORTH BRITISH LOCOMOTIVE COMPANY LIMITED
in February 1912
Reprinted in 1970 by
DAVID & CHARLES (PUBLISHERS) LIMITED
South Devon House Railway Station
Newton Abbot Devon

Printed in Great Britain by
Redwood Press Limited London and Trowbridge

INTRODUCTION TO THE 1970 REPRINT

It was in 1860 that Walter Montgomerie Neilson decided to move his flourishing but small locomotive factory from the Stobcross district of Glasgow to the rural northern suburb of Springburn. Springburn already had a railway tradition. The Cowlairs works of the Edinburgh & Glasgow and the St Rollox works of the Caledonian were already established there.

The new works were given the name of the street in which the original factory had stood; Hyde Park. The planning of the works was the work of Henry Dübs and Sampson George Goodall Copestake, Neilson's works manager and chief draughtsman. But immediately on the completion of the works Dübs and Copestake resigned from Neilsons and built their own locomotive works—the Glasgow Locomotive Works—at Polmadie on the south side of the city.

Neilson, faced with the loss of his two key men, nevertheless attracted two equally eminent men to fill their places. James Reid became his managing partner and Edward Snowball, who had trained under Robert Stephenson, his chief draughtsman. James Reid, a powerful personality, dominated the firm; so much so that in 1884, following a quarrel, Walter Neilson left the business and Reid became sole proprietor. The style Neilson & Co was retained at Hyde Park, and it was not until 1897 that the Reid family got its name in the title; Neilson, Reid & Co.

Neilson, with strong financial and technical support built his own works a very easy stone throw from Hyde Park—the Clyde Locomotive Works. But within three years the establishment was in distress. The almost new factory was bought by Sharp Stewart & Co Ltd in 1887 who gave it the name of their Manchester factory—Atlas Works.

The three great Glasgow locomotive works operated independently until 1903. (On 31 December 1899, of the 13,532 men employed by the ten leading British locomotive builders 6,851 worked for the Glasgow firms.) In 1903, American competition in overseas markets forced the three companies to amalgamate to form the North British Locomotive Company Limited, the largest locomotive building concern in Europe. Fifty years later, at its jubilee in 1953, the NBL had 28,000 engines to its credit and great things were promised for the future. But the world-wide eclipse of steam, and the tendency of traditional NBL markets to build their own engines led to a quick decline and the total demise of the great locomotive-building empire by 1962.

JOHN THOMAS

NOTES

These notes by Alan Dunbar give available details of which locomotives were built at which works, the works number, and the customer. They are to be read in conjuction with the index on pages 13 and 14.

The reference number is the NBL Order Number which was prefixed by the letter L. The letters in the last column indicate the works at which the engines were built, ie H=Hyde Park, Q=Queens Park, A=Atlas.

L2	1903	Kensei Rly	16019–20	Q	Japan
L12	1903	Natal Govt Rly	16060–84	Q	
L14	1903	Cape Govt Rly	16095–102	H	
L21	1903	,, ,, ,,	16161–70	H	
L26	1903	Madras & Southern Mahratta	16185–9	A	
L28	1903	Natal Govt Rly	16192–3	Q	
L29	1903	Central South African	16193–203	H	
L31	1903	,, ,, ,,	16207	H	
L33	1903	Tal-Tal Rly	16209–10	Q	Chile
L44	1903	Egyptian War Office	16302–16	H	
L49	1903	Hokkaido (Kansan) Rly	16342–7	Q	Japan
L58	1904	Madras Rly	16429–32	A	
L64	1904	South African Mines	16447	A	
L67	1904	Madras Rly	16464–5	Q	
L108	1905	Imperial Japanese Rlys	16735–52	H	
L116	1905	Burma Rly	16824–32	H	
L118	1905	Great Western	16853–7	Q	Brazil
L120	1905	Egyptian Delta	16860–5	A	
L135	1905	Bengal-Nagpur	16967–72	A	
L144	1905	,, ,,	17108–13	A	
L149	1905	South Indian	17198–207	A	
L152	1905	Queensland Govt	17224–5	Q	
L153	1905	Great Western	17226–31	Q	Brazil
L163	1905	Rio Tinto Mines	17303–4	H	
L164	1905	Assam-Bengal	17305–14	H	
L172	1906	Cordoba Central	17347–57	H	
L173	1906	,, ,,	17358–67	H	
L178	1906	Southern Rly	17401–9	A	Spain
L179	1906	Manilla Rly	17410–14	Q	
L181	1906	South Indian	17433–5	Q	
L196	1906	Cape Govt	17600	H	
L203	1906	Cordoba Central	17669–701	H	
L204	1906	,, ,,	17702–20	Q	
L205	1906	,, ,,	17721–24	Q	
L206	1906	Kensei Rly	17725–6	Q	Japan
L208	1906	Madras & South Mahratta	17734–38	H	
L224	1906	Soudan Govt	17853–62	H	
L228	1906	Great Western	17898–903	Q	Brazil
L230	1906	Indian State	17905–10	H	Jodhpur-Bikander
L240	1907	Rio Tinto Mines	18023–34	Q	
L254	1907	Bengal-Nagpur	18101–33	H	
L255	1907	,, ,,	18134–9	H	
L256	1907	,, ,,	18140–5	A	
L271	1907	Lantaro Nitrate	18312	A	

L275	1907	Rio Tinto	18320–23	Q	
L279	1907	Assam-Bengal	18338–45	H	
L282	1907	Cordoba Central	18375–6	A	
L284	1907	Imperial Teisan	18378–82	Q	Japan
L285	1907	,, ,,	18383–4	H	,,
L287	1907	Great Western	18387–92	H	Brazil
L295	1908	Vasco Asturian	18447–8	Q	Spain
L300	1908	Nigerian Rlys	18511–15	H	
L313	1908	Samana Y Santiago	18636–7	H	
L316	1908	Bengal-Nagpur	18654–7	A	
L319	1908	Burma Mines	18672–4	A	
L331	1908	Ceylon Rlys	18778–81	A	
L332	1908	Kalka-Simla	18782–90	H	India
L334	1908	Buenos Aires Midi	18793–802	H	
L350	1909	Sierra Mineral	18918–19	A	
L356	1909	Manilla Rly	18950–4	Q	
L359	1909	South African	18971–80	H	
L368	1909	Sierra Mineral	19018	A	
L371	1909	South Indian	19022–5	Q	
L378	1909	Natal Govt	19051–71	Q	
L381	1909	Argentine Govt*	19084	A	
L384	1909	Burma Rly	19117–120	Q	
L385	1909	Bengal-Nagpur	19121–23	A	
L387	1909	Leopoldina Rly	19127–32	Q	
L392	1909	Rohilkund & Kumson	19152–4	Q	
L398	1910	South African	19195–206	H	Class 100
L400	1910	,, ,,	19217–241	H	,, 3
L401	1910	,, ,,	19242–3	A	,, 4
L405	1910	Nigerian Rlys	19263–5	H	
L410	1910	Argentine Govt	19298–307	H	
L414	1910	Rhodesian Rlys	19317–9	H	
L416	1910	Sierra Mineral	19321–2	A	
L418	1910	Madras & South Mahratta	19325–7	Q	
L419	1910	Soudan Govt	19328–31	A	
L420	1910	,, ,,	19332–4	H	
L424	1910	Benguella Rly	19348–52	A	
L426	1910	South African	19355	H	Class ME
L430	1910	Oficina Mario	19371–2	H	
L431	1910	Manilla Rly	19373–7	Q	
L432	1910	Argentine Govt	19378–402	H	
L434	1910	Antofagasta	19428–35	H	
L445	1911	North Western	19560–3	A	Peru
L446	1911	Imperial Rly	19564–75	Q	Japan
L447	1911	Emu Bay Rly	19576	Q	Tasmania
L448	1911	South African	19577–586	Q	Class MO
L450	1911	,, ,,	19593–6	A	,, 12
L451	1911	,, ,,	19597–601	A	,, 3

*Originally built as stock

NOTES

Engines built by Neilson previous to amalgamation

The letter E was used as a prefix to the Order Number by Neilson and Sharp Stewart. (Dubs used the first Progress Number as the Order Number with the letter E as a suffix. The NBL in their records indicated this as D3999E.)

E601	1886	Indian State Rly	3554–83	Neilson	
E611	1887	West Australian	3630–1	,,	
E613	1887	Samana Y Santiago	3642	,,	
E614	1887	Bengal North West	3643–6	,,	
E622	1888	New Zealand Govt	3751	,,	
E627	1888	Emu Bay Rly	3765	,,	Tasmania
E645	1889	Manilla Rly	3893–3907	,,	
E666	1890	Sango Japan	4150–63	,,	
E676	1891	Costa Rica	4291–3	,,	
E698	1892	Cape Govt	4481–5	,,	South Africa
E703	1893	Donegal Rly	4573–8	,,	Ireland
E707	1893	Assam-Bengal	4617–24	,,	
E708	1893	Perah Govt	4625–6	,,	
E713	1893	Nippon Rly	4656–7	,,	Japan
E714	1893	,, ,,	4658–65	,,	,,
E719	1894	Bombay-Baroda	4678–81	,,	
E740	1895	West Australian	4833–9	,,	
E744	1895	Norway State	4858–9	,,	
E757	1896	West Australian	4932–6	,,	
E758	1896	,, ,,	4937–41	,,	
E764	1896	Cordoba Central	5068–70	,,	
E772	1896	Egypt	5092–3	,,	
E788	1898	Bombay Baroda	5324–6	,,	
E796	1897	Cape Govt	5282–7	,,	
E797	1898	Uganda Railway	5288–93	,,	
E820	1899	Cork & Blackrock	5561–4	,,	Ireland
E855	1901	Cape Govt	5867–70	,,	
E858	1900	South African Govt*	5897–902	,,	
E868	1900	Cape Govt	6079–88	,,	
E870	1900	Donegal Rly	6103–4	,,	
E871	1901	Perah State	6105–10	,,	
E874	1901	Bengal North West	6115–34	,,	
E875	1901	Rohilkund Rly	6135	,,	
E878	1901	Natal Govt	6158–67	,,	
E887	1902	Bengal North West	6254–83	,,	
E893	1902	Cape Govt	15888–9	,,	
E903	1903	New Cape Central	15903–4	,,	

*Supplied for 'military purposes', and probably utilised during the Boer War.

The above list concludes the engines shown in the Catalogue as built by Messrs Neilson at Hyde Park Works. It will be noted that the final orders in 1902–3 carried calculated numbers from the NBL list.

Engines built by Sharp, Stewart & Co, Atlas Works, Glasgow

None of the engines shown in the Catalogue were built at their Manchester works; all were Glasgow-built.

E917	Amorevita & Guernica	3433–5	1887	
E927	Mogzara Rly	3479–83	1888	
E932	,, ,,	3484–5	,,	
E938	North Central	3528–9*	1888	Argentine
E939	,, ,,	3530–56	1888	,,
E941	Darjeeling Rly	3516–9	1888	
E949	Cadagua Rly	3583–4	1888	
E957	Mogzara Rly	3643–4	1889	
E969	Cordoba North West	3624–5/3666–9	1889/1890	
E981	Marica Rly	3698	1890	
E1006	Mogzara Rly	3876–7	1892	
E1023	Glasgow Corporation	3940–4†	1893	Gas Dept
E1030	Jas Jenkins & Co	3980–1	1893	For Spain
E1037	Kieskui Rly	4014–5	1894	
E1040	Robla & Almasuda	4016–20	1894	
E1068	Java State	4136–7	1895	
E1081	Howrah Rly	4170–3	1895	
E1088	Tasmanian Govt	4189	1896	
E1092	Imperial Japanese	4241–2	1896	
E1095	Selangor Rly	4267–8	1896	
E1114	Nippon Rly	4433–8	1897	
E1132	New Zealand Govt	4508–11	1898	
E1158	Selta Cullera Rly	4633	1899	
E1173	New Zealand Govt	4745–54	1900	
E1178	Demerara Rly	4708–9	1900	
E1185	Howrah Rly	4826–7	1901	
E1186	Ceylon Govt	4822–5	1901	
E1187	Delhi-Kalka Rly	4914–23	1902	
E1188	Bengal-Nagpur	4872–81	1901	
E1189	Rohilkund Rly	4928–37	1901	
E1195	Agafera Hellen	4871	1901	
E1197	Behar Rly	4925–7	1901	
E1199	Cape Govt	4969–76	1902	
E1201	Bahia Govt	4740–1	1902	
E1208	Leopoldina Rly	15863–7	1903	

*Von Borries Compound

†2′ 6″ Gauge

Administration Building, Pediment on Front Entrance

North British Locomotive Company, Limited

Glasgow, Scotland

∵

CATALOGUE OF NARROW GAUGE LOCOMOTIVES

The North British Locomotive Company, Limited

HYDE PARK WORKS — QUEEN'S PARK WORKS — ATLAS WORKS

GLASGOW

DIRECTORS.

WILLIAM LORIMER, LL.D., Chairman.
HUGH REID, Deputy Chairman and Chief Managing Director.
ANDREW T. REID, WM. LORIMER, Jr., and JOHN H. SHARP, Managing Directors.
J. F. ROBINSON, JOHN REID, WALTER M. N. REID, and A. S. LORIMER.

Joint Secretaries—B. WINCHESTER and GEO. B. SAWERS.

HEAD OFFICE AND ADMINISTRATION BUILDINGS, SPRINGBURN, GLASGOW

TELEGRAMS: "LOCO GLASGOW"

"ENGINEERING STANDARDS CODE," "ABC CODE" 5th Ed., LIEBER'S CODE, WESTERN UNION CODE

The Company was formed in 1903 by the amalgamat.on of the three well-known firms:

MESSRS. NEILSON REID & CO., Hyde Park Locomotive Works, Glasgow.
MESSRS. DUBS & CO., Glasgow Locomotive Works, Glasgow.
MESSRS. SHARP, STEWART & CO., LTD., Atlas Works, Glasgow.

The Three Works are, as stated above, situated within the City of Glasgow, perhaps the most famous centre of Engineering and Shipbuilding activity in the world.

Their history as separate concerns extends back for over three-quarters of a century, and their Engines have been supplied to practically every Country in the world.

The combined output is now over 19,000 Engines, and the three Works, greatly enlarged and equipped throughout with the finest modern Machine Tools, are at present capable of turning out, per annum, over 700 Main Line Locomotives in the highest grade of British workmanship, and to the British Engineering Standard Specifications.

LONDON AGENTS and OFFICE, MESSRS. BROWNING & BERTRAM, 17 VICTORIA ST, WESTMINSTER.—Telegrams: "Hypar London"

ARGENTINA - - - - -	MESSRS. FRANKLIN & HERRERA, LTD., Buenos Ayres
AUSTRALIA - - - - -	MESSRS. GILBERT LODGE & CO., Sydney
WESTERN AUSTRALIA - -	MR. JOHN DENNY, Perth
CHINA - - - - - -	MESSRS. JARDINE MATHESON & CO., Hong Kong and Shanghai
CHILI - - - - - -	DON DOMINGO MERRY DEL VAL, Santiago
SPAIN - - - - - -	MESSRS. SHELDON GOENAGA & CO., Bilbao
PORTUGAL - - - -	MR. A. W. PATERSON, Lisbon

—— FEBRUARY, 1912. ——

North British Locomotive Company, Limited

GLASGOW

"HIBERNIA"
Liverpool and Manchester Railway, 1834

London Exhibition, 1862

HISTORICAL NOTE

WITH the success of "The Rocket" in the famous Rainhill Competition of 1829, there was inaugurated the important industry of Locomotive-Engine Manufacture. Hitherto the Locomotive had merely formed an item in the mixed production of General Engineering Workshops. At this stage specialization began to take place.

1828-1887

In Manchester, **Sharp, Roberts & Co.,** Manufacturers of Cotton Spinning Machinery now undertook the production of Machine Tools specially adapted for Locomotive Work, and in the year 1834 they made their first delivery of Locomotives, viz.—No. 1, an experimental Engine for the Liverpool and Manchester Railway, and Nos. 2 ("Hibernia"), 3 and 4 for the Dublin and Kingstown Railway. In 1843 the name of the firm was changed to Sharp Brothers & Co., and in 1852 there was assumed the style of

SHARP, STEWART & CO.,
ATLAS WORKS, MANCHESTER

1832-1897

In Glasgow, at the same time, **Neilson & Co.,** Hyde Park Street, had commenced building Stationary and Marine Engines, and, a few years later, they had added Locomotive Engines to their list of manufactures. In 1860, the Works in Hyde Park Street had become quite unsuitable for their extensive trade in Locomotives, and there was established in Springburn the firm of

NEILSON & CO.,
HYDE PARK LOCOMOTIVE WORKS, GLASGOW

1864-1903

In 1864 there was founded on the South Side of Glasgow the firm of

DUBS & CO., GLASGOW LOCOMOTIVE WORKS, GLASGOW

1887-1903

In 1887 **Sharp, Stewart & Co., Ltd.,** acquired the Works of the Clyde Locomotive Co., Ltd., Springburn, Glasgow, and removing to them from Manchester, became

SHARP, STEWART & CO., LTD.,
ATLAS WORKS, GLASGOW

1897-1903

In 1897 the style of the firm of **Neilson & Co.** was changed to

NEILSON, REID & CO.,
HYDE PARK LOCOMOTIVE WORKS, GLASGOW

In 1903, by the Amalgamation of the three firms, there was formed the

NORTH BRITISH LOCOMOTIVE COMPANY, LIMITED, GLASGOW

ADMINISTRATION BUILDING

OF THE

NORTH BRITISH LOCOMOTIVE COMPANY, LTD.

FORMALLY OPENED BY THE

RIGHT HON. THE EARL OF ROSEBERY, K.G., K.T., P.C.

10TH SEPTEMBER, 1909

QUADRANGLE—WEST FRONT

ADMINISTRATION BUILDING

OF THE

NORTH BRITISH LOCOMOTIVE COMPANY, LTD.

HYDE PARK WORKS **QUEEN'S PARK WORKS** **ATLAS WORKS**

The Three Works are Completely Equipped as Independent Units

The Erecting Shop at Hyde Park Works

The Erecting Shop at Queen's Park Works

The Erecting Shop at Atlas Works

HYDE PARK WORKS **QUEEN'S PARK WORKS** **ATLAS WORKS**

The Boiler Shop at Atlas Works

The Forge at Queen's Park Works

The Light Turning Shop at Hyde Park Works

CATALOGUE OF
Locomotives for Narrow Gauge Railways

The **Locomotive Engines and Tenders,** recently constructed for Narrow Gauge Railways, illustrated herein, form a selection, from the Company's lists, of those considered most suitable for general requirements.

They have been subjected to the practical test of everyday working on important Colonial and Foreign Railways, such as the **Government Railways of India, Ceylon, Australia, South Africa and New Zealand,** the **State Railways of Japan and Argentina,** and the railways of **Brazil, Chili, Manila, etc.**

Drawings, Patterns, Templates and Special Tools are in stock, and the manufacture of these Engines can therefore be undertaken under the **most favourable conditions for clients** in respect of **Price and Delivery.**

Enquiries regarding Engines to **special designs and specifications,** or to fulfil certain **Traffic requirements,** will always receive most careful consideration, and Quotations, if desired, will be submitted by the Company.

INDEX No. 1

Gauge, Type, Cylinders, Coupled Wheels

3 ft. 6 in. Gauge. Engines with Tenders

Type.	Page.	Ref. No.	Cylinders.	Wheels (Coup.).
2.6.6.2	16	L426	(4) 15″ × 23″	3′ 6¼″
2.6.6.0	16	L448	(4) 17½″ & 28″ × 26″	3′ 9½″
4.6.2	17	L398	18″ × 26″	4′ 9″
,,	17	L419	18″ × 24″	4′ 6″
,,	18	L359a	20″ × 28″	5′ 2″
,,	18	L359	18½″ × 28″	5′ 2″
,,	18	L29	18½″ × 28″	5′ 2″
,,	18	L28	19″ × 24″	4′ 3″
,,	19	L196	(3) 19″, 19″, 21½″ × 26″	5′ 0″
,,	19	L453	17″ × 23″	4′ 6″
4.8.2	20	L400	21″ × 24″	3′ 9½″
,,	20	L401	20½″ × 28″	4′ 6″
,,	20	L450	22½″ × 26″	4′ 3″
,,	20	L451	22″ × 24″	3′ 9½″
2.8.2	20	L31	20″ × 26″	4′ 0″
4.4.2	21	L179	16″ × 24″	5′ 0″
2.4.0	21	E1068	15″ × 18″	4′ 8½″
0.4.2	21	E772	13″ × 20″	3′ 9″
4.4.0	21	E666	15½″ × 22″	4′ 6″
,,	22	E1199	17½″ × 24″	5′ 0″
,,	22	3657E	17″ × 23″	4′ 6″
,,	22	3958E	16″ × 24″	5′ 0″
,,	22	E796	16″ × 24″	4′ 6″
,,	23	L285	16″ × 22″	4′ 6″
,,	23	3431E	16″ × 22″	4′ 9″
,,	23	E1114	16″ × 22″	4′ 6″
,,	23	3665E	15″ × 22″	4′ 1″
,,	23	3236E	(2) 12⅝″ & 18⅞″ × 18″	4′ 7″
4.6.0	24	L446	17½″ × 24″	5′ 3″
,,	24	E893	18½″ × 26″	4′ 6″
,,	24	L420	18″ × 24″	4′ 3″
,,	25	E1173	16″ × 22″	4′ 1″
,,	25	L44	17″ × 22″	4′ 6″
,,	25	L424	17″ × 26″	4′ 6″
,,	26	L224	17″ × 23″	4′ 6″
,,	26	2664E	16″ × 24″	3′ 10″
,,	26	E676	15″ × 20″	3′ 6″
,,	26	2483E	15″ × 20″	3′ 3″
,,	27	3413E	14½″ × 20″	3′ 3″
0.6.2	27	4304E	18½″ × 24″	4′ 7″
2.6.2	27	E855	18″ × 26″	4′ 6″
2.6.0	28	L49	17″ × 22″	4′ 0″
,,	28	L206	17″ × 22″	4′ 0″
,,	28	E714	17″ × 22″	4′ 0″
,,	28	E713	(2) 17″ & 25″ × 32″	4′ 0″
,,	29	E744	13⅞″ × 18⅛″	3′ $5\frac{11}{32}$″
,,	29	3385E	14″ × 20″	3′ 6″
,,	29	E740	14½″ × 20″	3′ 3″
,,	29	2893E	12″ × 20″	3′ 3″
4.8.0	30	L414	19″ × 24″	4′ 0″
,,	30	E1132	16″ × 22″	3′ 6¼″
,,	30	L461	17″ × 23″	3′ 6½″
,,	30	L447	17½″ × 22″	3′ 9″

3 ft. 6 in. Gauge. Engines with Tenders—*Continued*

Type.	Page.	Ref. No.	Cylinders.	Wheels (Coup.).
4.8.0	31	L378	20½″ × 24″	3′ 9½″
,,	31	L300	17″ × 23″	3′ 6¾″
,,	31	L21	18½″ × 24″	4′ 0″
,,	31	E903	17″ × 23″	3′ 6¼″
,,	31	E868	17½″ × 23″	3′ 7¼″
2.8.0	32	L14	18½″ × 24″	4′ 0″
,,	32	E757	15½″ × 21″	3′ 0″

3 ft. 6 in. Gauge. Tank Engines

Type.	Page.	Ref. No.	Cylinders.	Wheels (Coup.).
4.4.4	33	E758	15½″ × 21″	4′ 0″
0.4.0	33	E698	10″ × 20″	3′ 2″
4.4.0	33	2703E	15″ × 22″	4′ 1″
2.4.2	34	L284	14″ × 20″	4′ 1″
,,	34	4009E	14″ × 20″	4′ 4″
,,	34	2765E	13″ × 18″	4′ 0″
,,	34	E1178	13″ × 18″	4′ 6″
,,	35	3174E	11″ × 18″	3′ 9⅛″
,,	35	E645	13″ × 18″	4′ 6″
,,	35	E613	9½″ × 18″	3′ 0″
0.6.0	36	L64	16″ × 20″	3′ 3″
,,	36	L240	17″ × 22″	3′ 3″
,,	36	L275	15″ × 22″	3′ 0″
,,	37	3324E	15″ × 22″	4′ 0″
,,	37	E1037	15″ × 20″	4′ 0″
,,	37	3263E	14″ × 20″	3′ 9″
,,	37	3420E	14″ × 18″	3′ 0″
,,	37	E1092	13″ × 18″	3′ 0″
,,	37	2419E	13″ × 18″	3′ 0″
,,	38	L405	13″ × 18″	3′ 3½″
,,	38	E622	10½″ × 18″	3′ 0½″
,,	38	L163	12¼″ × 18″	3′ 0″
,,	38	E611	9″ × 14″	2′ 4″
0.6.2	39	L108	16″ × 24″	4′ 1″
,,	39	L2	16″ × 24″	4′ 0″
,,	39	L431	13″ × 18″	3′ 4½″
,,	39	L271	13″ × 20″	3′ 1″
2.6.0	40	L33	14½″ × 20″	3′ 3″
0.6.4	40	3182E	16″ × 20″	3′ 3″
,,	40	E627	13″ × 18″	3′ 1″
4.6.0	40	2317E	14″ × 20″	3′ 9″
4.6.4	41	E878	15″ × 22″	3′ 2″
2.6.2	41	2179E	15″ × 20″	3′ 3″
,,	41	L313	12″ × 18″	3′ 0″
,,	41	3172E	11″ × 18″	3′ 0″
4.8.2	42	L12	18″ × 22″	3′ 6″
,,	42	3317E	17″ × 21″	3′ 3″
2.8.4	42	E858	17″ × 21″	3′ 2″
4.6.2	43	L356	16″ × 24″	4′ 0″
,,	43	3653E	17″ × 23″	4′ 6″
4.10.2	43	3835E	19″ × 27″	3′ 9″

INDEX No. 1—*Continued*

Metre Gauge. Engines with Tenders

TYPE.	PAGE.	REF. NO.	CYLINDERS.	WHEELS (COUP.).
0.6.6.0	46	L384	(4) 15½″ & 24¼″ × 20″	3′ 3″
,,	46	L418	(4) 15½″ & 24¼″ × 20″	3′ 3″
,,	46	L350	(4) 18″ & 28″ × 24″	3′ 9″
,,	46	L416	(4) 17″ & 26½″ × 24″	3′ 9″
4.4.0	47	L153	16″ × 20″	4′ 8″
,,	47	E764	16″ × 22″	4′ 9″
,,	47	E938	(2) 15″ & 21½″ × 22″	4′ 6″
,,	48	L149	14″ × 20″	4′ 5″
,,	48	E601	14″ × 20″	4′ 5″
,,	48	E1095	14″ × 20″	4′ 3″
,,	48	E957	13″ × 16″	3′ 7½″
,,	49	3312E	14″ × 20″	3′ 6″
,,	49	E708	12″ × 18″	3′ 3″
2.4.0	49	E719	13″ × 20″	3′ 6″
2.4.2	49	L230	13″ × 20″	3′ 6½″
4.4.2	49	L205	17″ × 24″	4′ 9″
0.6.0	50	E797	14½″ × 20″	3′ 6½″
,,	50	L392	14″ × 20″	3′ 7″
,,	51	L26	14″ × 20″	3′ 6½″
2.6.0	50	L287	16″ × 20″	3′ 6″
4.6.2	51	L204	18″ × 24″	4′ 0″
,,	51	L173	18″ × 22″	4′ 6″
4.6.0	51	L334	16″ × 22″	4′ 0″
,,	52	L255	15½″ × 22″	4′ 9″
,,	52	L116	15½″ × 22″	4′ 9″
,,	53	L254	15″ × 22″	4′ 0″
,,	53	L279	15″ × 22″	4′ 0″
,,	54	E874	15″ × 22″	5′ 0″
,,	54	E887	15″ × 22″	4′ 0″
,,	54	E1189	14½″ × 20″	4′ 0″
,,	55	L282	15¼″ × 18″	3′ 4″
,,	55	L387	15″ × 22″	4′ 4″
,,	55	E871	14½″ × 20″	4′ 3½″
,,	55	3220E	14″ × 20″	3′ 3″
,,	55	E927	14″ × 18″	3′ 4″
,,	55	E969	14″ × 18″	3′ 4″
2.8.0	56	L228	15″ × 18″	3′ 1″
,,	56	E939	(2) 16″ & 23″ × 24″	3′ 6″
,,	56	E1208	15″ × 18″	3′ 1″
2.8.2	57	L432	17″ × 22 1/16″	3′ 6″
4.8.0	57	L178	19″ × 24″	3′ 9″
,,	58	L381	(2) 18″ & 26″ × 22″	3′ 6″
,,	58	L203	18″ × 22″	3′ 6″
,,	58	L118	18″ × 22″	3′ 6″
,,	59	L164	16″ × 22″	3′ 7″
,,	59	L208	16″ × 22″	3′ 7″

Metre Gauge. Tank Engines

TYPE.	PAGE.	REF. NO.	CYLINDERS.	WHEELS (COUP.).
0.4.0	60	E614	12¼″ × 18″	3′ 0″
2.4.0	60	3044E	13″ × 20″	3′ 6″
,,	60	E1158	11″ × 18″	3′ 6″
2.4.2	60	E707	12″ × 18″	3′ 6″

Metre Gauge. Tank Engines—*Continued*

TYPE.	PAGE.	REF. NO.	CYLINDERS.	WHEELS (COUP.).
4.4.0	61	4345E	15½″ × 22″	4′ 3½″
,,	61	3338E	12″ × 18″	3′ 6″
,,	61	E949	14″ × 20″	4′ 0″
4.4.2	62	3621E	12″ × 18″	3′ 6″
4.4.4	62	L181	14″ × 20″	4′ 5″
0.6.2	62	L368	14¼″ × 20″	3′ 0″
,,	62	L172	16″ × 20″	3′ 9″
0.6.0	63	E917	13″ × 20″	3′ 1″
4.6.0	63	E1030	12″ × 18″	3′ 0″
,,	63	3156E	14″ × 20″	3′ 3″
2.6.2	63	3170E	14″ × 20″	3′ 6″
,,	63	E1040	14½″ × 18″	3′ 6″
,,	64	L256	15″ × 22″	3′ 7″
,,	64	L295	16″ × 20″	3′ 3″
,,	64	4221E	16″ × 20″	3′ 3″
,,	65	E1006	15¼″ × 18″	3′ 4″
,,	65	3932E	14½″ × 20″	3′ 3″
,,	65	E1201	14½″ × 18″	3′ 0″
,,	65	4229E	14½″ × 20″	3′ 3″
2.8.4	65	L410	19″ × 20″	3′ 6″

3 ft. 0 in. Gauge. Engines with Tenders

TYPE.	PAGE.	REF. NO.	CYLINDERS.	WHEELS (COUP.).
4.8.0	69	L445	17″ × 20″	3′ 3″
4.6.0	69	2571E	16″ × 22″	4′ 0″

3 ft. 0 in. Gauge. Tank Engines

TYPE.	PAGE.	REF. NO.	CYLINDERS.	WHEELS (COUP.).
2.4.2	70	E820	14½″ × 22″	4′ 6″
4.4.4	70	E870	14″ × 20″	4′ 0″
0.6.2	69	2890E	15″ × 20″	4′ 0″
2.6.2	69	3169E	15″ × 20″	3′ 6″
4.6.0	70	E703	14″ × 20″	3′ 6″

2 ft. 6 in. Gauge. Engines with Tenders

TYPE.	PAGE.	REF. NO.	CYLINDERS.	WHEELS (COUP.).
4.6.2	71	L316	14½″ × 18″	3′ 6″
,,	71	L144	14½″ × 18″	3′ 6″
4.4.0	71	E981	11″ × 16″	3′ 4″
0.4.2	72	E788	10″ × 18″	3′ 0″
,,	72	E875	9″ × 14″	2′ 6″
2.8.0	72	L434	16½″ × 20″	3′ 1½″
2.8.2	72	L385	14½″ × 18″	2′ 10″

INDEX No. 1—*Continued*

2 ft. 6 in. Gauge. Tank Engines

TYPE.	PAGE.	REF. NO.	CYLINDERS.	WHEELS (COUP.).
0.4.0	73	L430	12″ × 16″	2′ 6″
0.4.2	73	E1187	12″ × 16″	2′ 6″
,,	73	E1186	11½″ × 14″	2′ 2″
,,	73	E1197	8″ × 14″	2′ 6″
4.6.4	74	L331	14″ × 20″	3′ 0″
0.6.4	74	L120	12″ × 16″	3′ 0½″
2.6.2	74	L332	14″ × 16″	2′ 6″
2.8.4	75	L135	14½″ × 18″	2′ 10″
,,	75	E1188	14½″ × 18″	2′ 10″
,,	75	L58	14″ × 18″	2′ 10″

2 ft. 0 in. Gauge. Engines with Tenders

TYPE.	PAGE.	REF. NO.	CYLINDERS.	WHEELS (COUP.).
0.6.0	76	L319	12″ × 16″	2′ 6″

2 ft. 0 in. Gauge. Tank Engines

TYPE.	PAGE.	REF. NO.	CYLINDERS.	WHEELS (COUP.).
0.4.0	77	E1195	6″ × 9″	1′ 8″
,,	77	E1023	6″ × 9″	1′ 8″
,,	77	E941	11″ × 14″	2′ 2″
,,	76	E1081	7″ × 12″	2′ 6″
2.4.2	77	E932	9″ × 14″	2′ 6″
0.4.2	77	E1088	12″ × 16″	2′ 6″
,,	76	E1185	8″ × 14″	2′ 6″

Pages 78–79 "ABT" Rack-Adhesion Engines.

INDEX No. 2

Gauge, Maximum and Average Weights, Type and Reference No.

NOTE.—The maximum weight per axle, as stated here, represents the engine as built and adjusted for the conditions of a particular railway.

1. In the great majority of cases it only represents the weight imposed by the "driving" axle. The *average weight* imposed by the coupled axles is therefore also stated.
2. In the case of engines with front and hind carrying wheels, such as the 2.4.2, 4.6.2, etc., types, the maximum weight may be decreased to the adhesive limit or increased to give a greater margin of adhesion.

3 ft. 6 in. Gauge. Engines with Tenders

MAXIMUM WEIGHT PER AXLE.	AVERAGE WEIGHT PER COUP. AXLE.	TYPE.	REF. NO.	PAGE.
Tons.	Tons.			
5·15	5·02	2.6.0	2893E	29
6·6	6·03	2.6.0	E744	29
6·81	6·7	4.4.0	3236E	23
6·91	6	2.6.0	3385E	29
7·25	7·07	0.4.2	E772	21
7·27	7·02	4.6.0	2483E	26
7·55	7·25	2.6.0	E740	29
7·82	7·03	4.6.0	3413E	27
7·87	7·82	2.4.0	E1068	21
7·95	7·5	4.6.0	E676	26
7·95	7·81	2.8.0	E757	32
7·95	7·91	4.8.0	E1132	30
9·05	9	4.8.0	E903	31
9·4	9·17	4.6.0	E1173	25
9·45	9·42	4.8.0	L300	31
9·7	9·5	4.8.0	E868	31
9·86	9·39	4.8.0	L447	30
9·9	9·9	2.6.6.2	L426	16
10·1	9·7	4.6.0	2664E	26
10·2	10·12	4.4.0	1114E	23

3 ft. 6 in. Gauge. Engines with Tenders
Continued

MAXIMUM WEIGHT PER AXLE.	AVERAGE WEIGHT PER COUP. AXLE.	TYPE.	REF. NO.	PAGE.
Tons.	Tons.			
10·3	10·15	4.4.0	E666	21
10·4	10·07	4.4.0	3958E	22
10·52	10·36	4.4.0	3665E	23
10·75	10·64	4.4.2	L179	21
11·1	11·03	4.4.0	3431E	23
11·1	11·1	4.4.0	L285	23
11·2	10·6	4.8.0	L461	30
11·35	11·28	4.6.2	L419	17
11·85	11·8	4.8.0	L21	31
11·87	11·81	4.6.0	L424	25
11·9	11·9	4.6.2	L453	19
11·97	11·85	2.6.0	L206	28
12·05	11·94	4.8.0	L414	30
12·13	12·06	4.6.0	L446	24
12·3	12·28	4.6.0	L224	26
12·31	12·03	0.6.2	4304E	27
12·4	12·28	4.6.0	L44	25
12·6	12·18	2.6.0	E713	28
12·6	12	2.6.0	L49	28
12·85	12·78	4.4.0	3657E	22

3 ft. 6 in. Gauge. Engines with Tenders
Continued

MAXIMUM WEIGHT PER AXLE.	AVERAGE WEIGHT PER COUP. AXLE.	TYPE.	REF. NO.	PAGE.
Tons.	Tons.			
13	12·39	2.6.0	E714	28
13	12·85	2.8.0	L14	32
13·25	11·8	2.6.2	E855	27
13·45	12·89	4.6.0	E893	24
13·65	13·18	4.6.0	L420	24
13·75	13·38	4.4.0	E796	22
14	14	4.6.2	L398	17
14·45	14·07	4.8.0	L378	31
14·62	14·42	2.6.6.0	L448	16
14·65	13·7	4.6.2	L28	18
14·85	14·5	4.6.2	L196	19
14·9	14·7	4.6.2	L29	18
14·9	14·82	4.4.0	E1199	22
14·95	14·74	4.8.2	L400	20
15	14·8	4.8.2	L401	20
15·56	15·4	4.8.2	L451	20
15·7	15·66	4.6.2	L359a	18
15·75	15·46	2.8.2	L31	20
15·9	15·66	4.6.2	L359	18
16·95	16·7	4.8.2	L450	20

INDEX No. 2—*Continued*

3 ft. 6 in. Gauge. Tank Engines

Metre Gauge. Engines with Tenders

Metre Gauge. Engines with Tenders

Continued

Metre Gauge. Tank Engines

Metre Gauge. Tank Engines

Continued

3 ft. 0 in. Gauge. Engines with Tenders

3 ft. 0 in. Gauge. Tank Engines

2 ft. 6 in. Gauge. Engines with Tenders

INDEX No. 2—*Continued*

2 ft. 6 in. Gauge. Tank Engines

2 ft. 0 in. Gauge. Engines with Tenders

2 ft. 0 in. Gauge. Tank Engines

INDEX No. 3

Reference Nos. and Code Words

INDEX No. 3—*Continued*

Locomotives for the 3 ft. 6 in. Gauge

"Mallet" Locomotives with Tenders

3 ft. 6 in. Gauge

Reference No. **L 426.**

2.6.6.2. TYPE.

"Mallet" Articulated SIMPLE Locomotive with Tender

Reference No.	Code Word.	CYLINDERS.	WHEELS (Diam.).			WHEEL BASE.			Boiler Working Pressure.	HEATING SURFACES.				Grate Area.	Tractive Force at 75 % B.P.	ENGINE WEIGHT.		TENDER.		
		Diam. × Stroke.	Front.	Coupled.	Hind.	Rigid.	Engine.	E. and T.		Tubes.	Super Heater.	Firebox.	Total.			Ad-hesive.	Total.	Tank Capacity.	Fuel.	Weight Full.
									Lbs.	Sq. Ft.	Sq. Ft.	Sq. Ft.	Sq. Ft.	Sq. Ft.	Lbs.	Tons.	Tons.	Gals.	Cub. Ft.	Tons.
L426	ARENDSBLIK	15″ × 23″	2′ 6″	3′ 6¼″	2′ 6″	8′ 6″	38′ 3″	58′ 5½″	170	1340	346	115	1801	32	31,220	59·4	72·1	3000	270	37·6
L448	ARENARAIT	17½″ & 28″ × 26″	2′ 4½″	3′ 9½″	—	8′ 4″	33′ 5″	59′ 3″	200	2462	—	154	2616	42·5	42,000	86·55	95·3	4000	225	43·5

Tractive Force **L 448** taken at 60% B.P. (when working "Simple" at 80 % B.P. 56,000 lbs.).

Reference No. **L 448.**

2.6.6.0. TYPE.

"Mallet" Articulated COMPOUND Locomotive with Tender

4.6.2. Type

Locomotives with Tenders

3 ft. 6 in. Gauge

Reference No. **L 398.**

Reference No.	Code Word.	Cylinders.	Wheels (Diam.).			Wheel Base.			Boiler Working Pressure.	Heating Surfaces.				Grate Area.	Tractive Force at 75 % B.P.	Engine Weight.		Tender.		
		Diam. × Stroke.	Front.	Coupled.	Hind.	Rigid.	Engine.	E. and T.		Tubes.	Super Heater.	Firebox.	Total.			Adhesive.	Total.	Tank Capacity.	Fuel.	Weight Full.
									Lbs.	Sq. Ft.	Sq. Ft.	Sq. Ft.	Sq. Ft.	Sq. Ft.	Lbs.	Tons.	Tons.	Gals.	Cub. Ft.	Tons.
L398	Arenatiora	18″ × 26″	2′ 4½″	4′ 9″	2′ 9″	10′ 0″	28′ 7½″	51′ 6″	200	1783	—	125	1908	31·5	22,168	42	64·75	2600	225	34·8
L419	Arendator	18″ × 24″	2′ 4½″	4′ 6″	3′ 0″	10′ 0″	25′ 9″	52′ 8″	180	1127	283	110	1520	22·54	19,440	33·85	54·05	4000	320	45·85

Reference No. **L 419.**

4.6.2. Type

Locomotives with Tenders

3 ft. 6 in. Gaug

Reference Nos. **L 359** and **L 359A**.

Note.—**L 359A** is fitted with Superheater.

Reference No.	Code Word.	Cylinders.	Wheels (Diam.).			Wheel Base.			Boiler Working Pressure.	Heating Surfaces.				Grate Area.	Tractive Force at 75 % B.P.	Engine Weight.		Tender.		
		Diam.×Stroke.	Front.	Coupled.	Hind.	Rigid.	Engine.	E. and T.		Tubes.	Super Heater.	Firebox.	Total.			Ad-hesive.	Total.	Tank Capacity.	Fuel.	Weig Ful
									Lbs.	Sq. Ft.	Sq. Ft.	Sq. Ft.	Sq. Ft.	Sq. Ft.	Lbs.	Tons.	Tons.	Gals.	Cub. Ft.	Tons
L359	ARENACEOUS	18½″ × 28″	2′ 4½″	5′ 2″	2′ 9″	10′ 10″	30′ 2″	55′ 8⅛″	200	1714	—	128	1842	34·6	23,184	47	73·75	4000	400	49·2
L359A	ARENALEJO	20″ × 28″	2′ 4½″	5′ 2″	2′ 9″	10′ 10″	30′ 2″	55′ 8⅛″	180	1494	446	128	2068	34·6	24,387	47	74·45	4000	400	49·2
L29	ARDESCATIS	18½″ × 28″	2′ 4½″	5′ 2″	2′ 9″	10′ 10″	30′ 2″	56′ 4″	200	1714	—	128	1842	35	23,184	44·15	70·6	4000	400	49·3
L28	ARDESCAM	19″ × 24″	2′ 4½″	4′ 3″	2′ 6″	9′ 4″	27′ 10″	51′ 1⅜″	180	2094	—	120	2214	28	22,934	41	64	3225	240	38

Reference No. **L 29**.

Reference No. **L 28**.

.2. Type

Locomotives with Tenders

3 ft. 6 in. Gauge

Reference No. **L 196.**

3-Cylinder Compound Locomotive.

Reference No.	Code Word.	Cylinders.	Wheels (Diam.).			Wheel Base.			Boiler Working Pressure.	Heating Surfaces.			Grate Area.	Tractive Force at 75 % B.P.	Engine Weight.		Tender.		
		Diam. × Stroke.	Front.	Coupled.	Hind.	Rigid.	Engine.	E. and T.		Tubes.	Firebox.	Total.			Ad-hesive.	Total.	Tank Capacity.	Fuel.	Weight Full.
									Lbs.	Sq. Ft.	Sq. Ft.	Sq. Ft.	Sq. Ft.	Lbs.	Tons.	Tons.	Gals.	Cub. Ft.	Tons.
L196	Arecido	19″ & 21½″ × 26″	2′ 4½″	5′ 0″	2′ 9″	10′ 5″	28′ 9″	49′ 7⅝″	200	1469	114	1583	26·5	18,772	43·45	66·1	2920	240	33·45
L453	Arenerions	17″ × 23″	2′ 6″	4′ 6″	2′ 6″	11′ 0″	27′ 2″	47′ 0″	175	1294	126	1420	18·8	16,150	35·7	53·02	2200	250	30·57

Tractive Force **L 196** taken at 60% B.P.

Reference No. **L 453.**

Locomotives with Tenders

3 ft. 6 in. Gauge

Reference No. **L 400.** **4.8.2. TYPE**

Reference No.	Code Word.	Cylinders.	Wheels (Diam.).			Wheel Base.			Boiler Working Pressure.	Heating Surfaces.				Grate Area.	Tractive Force at 75 % B.P.	Engine Weight.		Tender.		
		Diam. × Stroke.	Front.	Coupled.	Hind.	Rigid.	Engine.	E. and T.		Tubes.	Super Heater.	Firebox.	Total.			Ad-hesive.	Total.	Tank Capacity.	Fuel.	Weight Full
									Lbs.	Sq. Ft.	Sq. Ft.	Sq. Ft.	Sq. Ft.	Sq. Ft.	Lbs.	Tons.	Tons.	Gals.	Cub. Ft.	Tons
L400	Arenatos	21″ × 24″	2′ 4½″	3′ 9½″	2′ 6″	8′ 6″	30′ 9″	55′ 8″	200	2582	—	136	2718	34	34,893	58·95	78·8	4000	330	43·0
L31	Ardescebat	20″ × 26″	2′ 6″	4′ 0″	2′ 6″	13′ 1½″	29′ 3″	55′ 8″	200	2136	—	142	2278	37	32,500	61·85	78·8	4000	400	49·3
L401	Arencadas	20½″ × 28″	2′ 4½″	4′ 6″	2′ 9″	9′ 7″	31′ 11″	57′ 8⅜″	180	2131	—	186	2317	37	29,417	59·1	82·1	3500	300	43·4
L450	Argentadas	22½″ × 26″	2′ 4½″	4′ 3″	2′ 9″	9′ 0″	31′ 7½″	58′ 1⅞″	180	2312	669	158	3139	40	34,842	66·7	91·8	4250	400	50·9
L451	Argentado	22″ × 24″	2′ 4½″	3′ 9½″	2′ 6″	8′ 6″	30′ 9″	55′ 8″	180	2154	617	135	2906	34	34,234	61·7	83·2	4000	330	43·5

Note.—**L 450** and **L 451** are fitted with Superheater and Piston-Valves and are otherwise represented generally by Photo. Ref. No. **L 400.**

Reference No. **L 31.** **2.8.2. TYPE**

Reference No. **L 401.** **4.8.2. TYPE**

Locomotives with Tenders

3 ft. 6 in. Gauge

Reference No. **E 666.** **4.4.0. TYPE.**

Reference No.	Code Word.	Cylinders.	Wheels (Diam.).			Wheel Base.			Boiler Working Pressure.	Heating Surfaces.			Grate Area.	Tractive Force at 75 % B.P.	Engine Weight.		Tender.		
		Diam. × Stroke.	Front.	Coupled.	Hind.	Rigid.	Engine.	E. and T.		Tubes.	Firebox.	Total.			Ad-hesive.	Total.	Tank Capacity.	Fuel.	Weight Full.
									Lbs.	Sq. Ft.	Sq. Ft.	Sq. Ft.	Sq. Ft.	Lbs.	Tons.	Tons.	Gals.	Cub. Ft.	Tons.
E666	Arengaseis	15½″ × 22″	2′ 4″	4′ 6″	—	6′ 6″	18′ 0″	38′ 0″	150	781	80	861	14·75	11,115	20·3	28 6	2000	135	22·5
L179	Areceremos	16″ × 24″	2′ 7½″	5′ 0″	3′ 4½″	12′ 0″	21′ 2″	43′ 6½″	180	973	107	1080	16·5	13,824	21·3	40·8	2500	180	32
E1068	Arestinado	15″ × 18″	2′ 7½″	4′ 8½″	—	7′ 5″	16′ 10½″	33′ 0″	142	550	55	605	11·45	7,636	15·65	20·6	1000	110	14
E772	Arenosos	13″ × 20″	—	3′ 9″	3′ 0″	11′ 0″	11′ 0″	25′ 3⅛″	130	618	47	665	11	7,042	14·15	19·35	1200	150	15·58

Reference No. **L 179.** **4.4.2. TYPE.**

Reference No. **E 1068.** **2.4.0. TYPE.**

Reference No. **E 772.** **0.4.2. TYPE.**

4.4.0. Type

Locomotives with Tenders

3 ft. 6 in. Gauge

Reference No. **E 1199.**

Reference No. **3657 E.**

Reference No.	Code Word.	Cylinders.	Wheels (Diam.).		Wheel Base.			Boiler Working Pressure.	Heating Surfaces.			Grate Area.	Tractive Force at 75 % B.P.	Engine Weight.		Tender.		
		Diam. × Stroke.	Front.	Coupled.	Rigid.	Engine.	E. and T.		Tubes.	Firebox.	Total.			Ad-hesive.	Total.	Tank Capacity.	Fuel.	Weight Full.
								Lbs.	Sq. Ft.	Sq. Ft.	Sq. Ft.	Sq. Ft.	Lbs.	Tons.	Tons.	Gals.	Cub. Ft.	Tons.
E1199	Arfavamos	17½″ × 24″	2′ 4½″	5′ 0″	7′ 6″	20′ 0⅛″	41′ 5½″	180	910	109	1019	18	16,537	29·65	42·1	2470	260	31·85
3657E	Argeloos	17″ × 23″	2′ 4½″	4′ 6″	9′ 0″	22′ 10½″	45′ 4¾″	160	893	93	986	26	14,771	25·55	39·05	3000	288	36·5
3958E	Argematum	16″ × 24″	2′ 6″	5′ 0″	8′ 4″	21′ 7″	38′ 6″	160	791	84	875	14	12,288	20·15	31·5	2000	135	23·2
E796	Arenques	16″ × 24″	2′ 4½″	4′ 6″	7′ 0″	19′ 5¾″	40′ 6⅛″	160	879	85	964	15·7	13,656	26·75	38·75	2200	240	28·6

Reference No. **3958 E.**

Reference No. **E 796.**

4.4.0. Type

Locomotives with Tenders

3 ft. 6 in. Gauge

Reference No. **L 285.**

Reference No. **3431 E.**

Reference No. **E 1114.**

Reference No.	Code Word.	Cylinders.	Wheels (Diam.).		Wheel Base.			Boiler Working Pressure.	Heating Surfaces.			Grate Area.	Tractive Force at 75 % B.P.	Engine Weight.		Tender.		
		Diam. × Stroke.	Front.	Coupled.	Rigid.	Engine.	E. and T.		Tubes.	Firebox.	Total.			Ad-hesive.	Total.	Tank Capacity.	Fuel.	Weight Full.
								Lbs.	Sq. Ft.	Sq. Ft.	Sq. Ft.	Sq. Ft.	Lbs.	Tons.	Tons.	Gals.	Cub. Ft.	Tons.
L285	Arelais	16″ × 22″	2′ 4″	4′ 6″	8′ 4″	21′ 7″	40′ 0″	160	899	98	997	17	12,515	22·2	33·5	2300	110	25·52
E1114	Aretalogum	16″ × 22″	2′ 4″	4′ 6″	8′ 4″	21′ 7″	38′ 0$\frac{1}{8}$″	150	771	79	850	14·25	11,733	20·25	31·3	2000	135	22·25
3431E	Argayar	16″ × 22″	2′ 4″	4′ 9″	6′ 6″	19′ 0″	42′ 8$\frac{1}{2}$″	160	820	80	900	16·6	11,857	22·07	31·4	2000	160	25·7
3665E	Argeloozer	15″ × 22″	2′ 4″	4′ 1″	7′ 0″	18′ 4$\frac{1}{2}$″	37′ 9″	130	689	67	756	13	9,849	20·7	29·8	1950	160	23·5
3236E	Arganholz	12$\frac{5}{8}$″ & 18$\frac{7}{8}$″ × 18″	2′ 0″	4′ 7″	6′ 3″	17′ 5″	30′ 6″	171	463	48	511	8·54	5,345	13·4	21·6	700	70	9

Tractive Force **3236 E** taken at 60% B.P.

Reference No. **3665 E.**

Reference No. **3236 E.**

4.6.0. Type

Locomotives with Tenders

3 ft. 6 in. Gauge

Reference No. **L 446.**

Reference No.	Code Word.	Cylinders.	Wheels (Diam.).		Wheel Base.			Boiler Working Pressure.	Heating Surfaces.				Grate Area.	Tractive Force at 75 % B.P.	Engine Weight.		Tender.		
		Diam. × Stroke.	Front.	Coupled.	Rigid.	Engine.	E. and T.		Tubes.	Super Heater.	Firebox.	Total.			Ad-hesive.	Total.	Tank Capacity.	Fuel.	Weight Full.
								Lbs.	Sq. Ft.	Sq. Ft.	Sq. Ft.	Sq. Ft.	Sq. Ft.	Lbs.	Tons.	Tons.	Gals.	Cub. Ft.	Tons.
L446	Arendsveer	$17\frac{1}{2}'' \times 24''$	2′ 9″	5′ 3″	13′ 6″	24′ 6″	—	180	1300	—	127	1427	20	15,750	36·17	48·32	—	—	—
E893	Areolares	$18\frac{1}{2}'' \times 26''$	$2'\ 4\frac{1}{2}''$	4′ 6″	11′ 4″	21′ 2″	$45'\ 5\frac{1}{2}''$	180	958	234	109	1301	18·75	22,235	38·65	52·35	3200	200	36
L420	Arendrog	$18'' \times 24''$	$2'\ 4\frac{1}{2}''$	4′ 3″	12′ 3″	22′ 9″	$50'\ 6\frac{1}{2}''$	180	1282	—	102	1384	23·6	20,590	39·55	51·35	4600	450	51·85

Reference No. **E 893.**

Reference No. **L 420.**

6.0. Type

Locomotives with Tenders

3 ft. 6 in. Gauge

Reference No. **E 1173.**

Reference No.	Code Word.	CYLINDERS.	WHEELS (Diam.).		WHEEL BASE.			Boiler Working Pressure.	HEATING SURFACES.			Grate Area.	Tractive Force at 75 % B.P.	ENGINE WEIGHT.		TENDER.		
		Diam. × Stroke.	Front.	Coupled.	Rigid.	Engine.	E. and T.		Tubes.	Firebox.	Total.			Ad-hesive.	Total.	Tank Capacity.	Fuel.	Weight Full.
								Lbs.	Sq. Ft.	Sq. Ft.	Sq. Ft.	Sq. Ft.	Lbs.	Tons.	Tons.	Gals.	Cub. Ft.	Tons.
E1173	ARETICHI	16″ × 22″	2′ 6″	4′ 1″	10′ 0″	21′ 3″	42′ 6⅛″	200	882	92	974	17	17,240	27·5	38·7	1700	160	21·95
L44	ARDESCENS	17″ × 22″	2′ 4½″	4′ 6″	11′ 6″	21′ 9″	47′ 0″	180	971	110	1081	17	15,895	36·85	49·05	2600	180	33·85
L424	ARENDSBEEN	17″ × 26″	2′ 4½″	4′ 6″	11′ 0″	20′ 3¾″	46′ 6¼″	160	1015	101	1116	16·62	16,700	35·43	46·83	2600	256	34·42

Reference No. **L 44.**

Reference No. **L 424.**

4.6.0. Type

Locomotives with Tenders

3 ft. 6 in. Gauge

Reference No. **L 224.**

Reference No. **2664 E.**

Reference No.	Code Word.	Cylinders.	Wheels (Diam.).		Wheel Base.			Boiler Working Pressure.	Heating Surfaces.			Grate Area.	Tractive Force at 75 % B.P.	Engine Weight.		Tender.		
		Diam. × Stroke.	Front.	Coupled.	Rigid.	Engine.	E. and T.		Tubes.	Firebox.	Total.			Ad-hesive.	Total.	Tank Capacity.	Fuel.	Weight Full.
								Lbs.	Sq. Ft.	Sq. Ft.	Sq. Ft.	Sq. Ft.	Lbs.	Tons.	Tons.	Gals.	Cub. Ft.	Tons.
L224	Arefaction	17″ × 23″	2′ 4½″	4′ 6″	11′ 6″	21′ 9″	50′ 0½″	180	971	105	1076	19	16,617	36·85	49	4000	400	44·6
2664E	Argamasais	16″ × 24″	2′ 4″	3′ 10″	10′ 0″	19′ 1⅜″	40′ 2⅜″	150	946	86	1032	16·18	15,026	29	36·9	1950	160	23·5
E676	Arengasen	15″ × 20″	2′ 3½″	3′ 6″	8′ 0″	16′ 10″	36′ 5¼″	150	718	62	780	12	12,050	22·5	29·97	1700	120	20·4
2483E	Argamandel	15″ × 20″	2′ 0½″	3′ 3″	7′ 6″	16′ 6″	34′ 7″	135	680	68	748	13·24	11,683	21·05	27·75	1500	95	18·25

Reference No. **E 676.**

Reference No. **2483 E.**

0*

Locomotives with Tenders

3 ft. 6 in. Gauge

Reference No. **4304 E.** **0.6.2. TYPE.**

Reference No.	Code Word.	Cylinders.	Wheels (Diam.).			Wheel Base.			Boiler Working Pressure.	Heating Surfaces.			Grate Area.	Tractive Force at 75 % B.P.	Engine Weight.		Tender.		
		Diam. × Stroke.	Front.	Coupled.	Hind.	Rigid.	Engine.	E. and T.		Tubes.	Firebox.	Total.			Ad-hesive.	Total.	Tank Capacity.	Fuel.	Weight Full.
									Lbs.	Sq. Ft.	Sq. Ft.	Sq. Ft.	Sq. Ft.	Lbs.	Tons.	Tons.	Gals.	Cub. Ft.	Tons.
3413E	Argayaba	14½″ × 20″	2′ 0″	3′ 3″	—	7′ 6″	15′ 10″	33′ 3½″	160	708	72	780	13·7	12,938	21·1	27·07	1560	212	21
4304E	Argennon	18½″ × 24″	—	4′ 7″	3′ 1½″	10′ 8″	18′ 11″	36′ 8¾″	160	1395	95	1490	24	17,920	36·1	43·6	2000	135	24·1
E855	Arenulae	18″ × 26″	2′ 4½″	4′ 6″	2′ 9″	9′ 10″	23′ 0″	45′ 9⅛″	180	1366	96	1462	25·5	21,060	35·4	51·85	2618	220	31·85

Reference No. **3413 E.** **4.6.0. TYPE.**

Reference No. **E 855.** **2.6.2. TYPE.**

2.6.0. Type

Locomotives with Tenders

3 ft. 6 in. Gaug

Reference No. **L 49.**

Reference No.	Code Word.	Cylinders.	Wheels (Diam.).		Wheel Base.			Boiler Working Pressure.	Heating Surfaces.			Grate Area.	Tractive Force at 75 % B.P.	Engine Weight.		Tender.		
		Diam. × Stroke.	Front.	Coupled.	Rigid.	Engine.	E. and T.		Tubes.	Firebox.	Total.			Adhesive.	Total.	Tank Capacity.	Fuel.	Weight Full.
								Lbs.	Sq. Ft.	Sq. Ft.	Sq. Ft.	Sq. Ft.	Lbs.	Tons.	Tons.	Gals.	Cub. Ft.	Tons.
L49	Ardescerem	17″ × 22″	2′ 6″	4′ 0″	12′ 6″	20′ 0″	41′ 0″	160	895	98	993	16	15,895	36·05	41·05	2500	130	27·5
L206	Areento	17″ × 22″	2′ 6″	4′ 0″	12′ 6″	20′ 0″	38′ 6″	140	895	96	991	16·6	13,908	35·55	40·5	2000	135	24·25
E714	Arenisco	17″ × 22″	2′ 6″	4′ 0″	12′ 6″	20′ 0″	39′ 0″	160	901	88	989	16·5	15,895	37·15	40·8	2000	135	23·05
E713	Arenilitic	17″ & 25″ × 22″	2′ 6″	4′ 0″	12′ 6″	20′ 3″	39′ 3″	180	901	88	989	16·5	14,305	36·55	41·6	2000	135	23·05

L 713 Tractive Force taken at 60% B.P.

Reference No. **L 206.**

Note.—Engine Tank Capacity, 430 Gallons.

Reference Nos. **E 714** (Simple).
E 713 (Compound).

Note.—Engine Tank Capacity, 700 Gallons.

.0. Type

Locomotives with Tenders

3 ft. 6 in. Gauge

Reference No. **E 744.**

Reference No.	Code Word.	CYLINDERS.	WHEELS (Diam.).		WHEEL BASE.			Boiler Working Pressure.	HEATING SURFACES.			Grate Area.	Tractive Force at 75 % B.P.	ENGINE WEIGHT.		TENDER.		
		Diam. × Stroke.	Front.	Coupled.	Rigid.	Engine.	E. and T.		Tubes.	Firebox.	Total.			Adhesive.	Total.	Tank Capacity.	Fuel.	Weight Full.
								Lbs.	Sq. Ft.	Sq. Ft.	Sq. Ft.	Sq. Ft.	Lbs.	Tons.	Tons.	Gals.	Cub. Ft.	Tons.
E744	ARENIVAGOS	$13\frac{7}{8}″ \times 18\frac{1}{8}″$	$2′\ 3\frac{9}{16}″$	$3′\ 5\frac{11}{32}″$	$11′\ 1\frac{3}{4}″$	$16′\ 11\frac{3}{4}″$	33′ 8″	142	562	58	620	10	8,988	18·1	22·55	990	120	13·45
3385E	ARGAVIESO	14″ × 20″	2′ 0″	3′ 6″	10′ 0″	15′ 10″	$33\ 4\frac{1}{2}″$	140	629	55	684	11·5	9,800	18	22·2	1200	100	15·2
E740	ARENIVAGI	$14\frac{1}{2}″ \times 20″$	2′ 0″	3′ 3″	7′ 6″	13′ 4″	$30′\ 9\frac{1}{2}″$	160	708	72	780	13·7	12,936	21·75	25·8	1550	212	18·7
2893E	ARGAMULA	12″ × 20″	2′ 0″	3′ 3″	7′ 6″	13′ 0″	28′ 8″	120	498	42	540	9·75	6,646	15·1	19·35	1600	90	17·3

Reference No. **3385 E.**

Reference No. **E 740.**

Reference No. **2893 E.**

4.8.0. Type

Locomotives with Tenders

3 ft. 6 in. Gaug

Reference No. **L 414.**

Reference No.	Code Word.	Cylinders.	Wheels (Diam.).		Wheel Base.			Boiler Working Pressure.	Heating Surfaces.			Grate Area.	Tractive Force at 75 % B.P.	Engine Weight.		Tender.		
		Diam. × Stroke.	Front.	Coupled.	Rigid.	Engine.	E. and T.		Tubes.	Firebox.	Total.			Adhesive.	Total.	Tank Capacity.	Fuel.	Weight. Full.
								Lbs.	Sq. Ft.	Sq. Ft.	Sq. Ft.	Sq. Ft.	Lbs.	Tons.	Tons.	Gals.	Cub. Ft.	Tons.
L414	Arencases	19″ × 24″	2′ 4½″	4′ 0″	9′ 0″	23′ 3″	48′ 4½″	180	1183	141	1324	21·35	24,367	47·75	60·7	3000	380	41·45
L461	Arengaban	17″ × 23″	2′ 6″	3′ 6½″	8′ 6″	22′ 11″	46′ 11¾″	175	1235	126	1361	18·8	20,528	42·45	54·1	2200	248	30·6
L447	Arendtang	17½″ × 22″	2′ 6″	3′ 9″	8′ 4″	22′ 0½″	43′ 8½″	175	1072	105	1177	16	19,635	37·55	47·53	2100	160	28·55
E1132	Areticaste	16″ × 22″	2′ 6″	3′ 6¼″	9′ 0″	23′ 6″	44′ 9⅛″	175	939	101	1040	17·5	17,495	31·65	42·15	1700	112	21·95

Reference No. **E 1132.**

Reference No. **L 461.**

Reference No. **L 447.**

8.0. Type

Locomotives with Tenders

3 ft. 6 in. Gauge

Reference No. **L 378.**

Reference No.	Code Word.	Cylinders. Diam. × Stroke.	Wheels (Diam.). Front.	Wheels (Diam.). Coupled.	Wheel Base. Rigid.	Wheel Base. Engine.	Wheel Base. E. and T.	Boiler Working Pressure.	Heating Surfaces. Tubes.	Heating Surfaces. Firebox.	Heating Surfaces. Total.	Grate Area.	Tractive Force at 75 % B.P.	Engine Weight. Adhesive.	Engine Weight. Total.	Tender. Tank Capacity.	Tender. Fuel.	Tender. Weight Full.
								Lbs.	Sq. Ft.	Sq. Ft.	Sq. Ft.	Sq. Ft.	Lbs.	Tons.	Tons.	Gals.	Cub. Ft.	Tons.
L378	Arenario	20½″ × 24″	2′ 4½″	3′ 9½″	8′ 6″	22′ 6″	50′ 3¼″	200	2005	132	2137	34	33,250	56·3	70·65	3500	240	40·2
L300	Arelanha	17″ × 23″	2′ 4½″	3′ 6¾″	8′ 0″	21′ 3½″	44′ 0″	170	976	112	1088	17·5	19,824	37·7	48·1	2000	150	25·12
E903	Areology	17″ × 23″	2′ 4″	3′ 6¼″	8′ 0″	21′ 3½″	46′ 2″	160	976	102	1078	17	18,878	36	46·7	2530	256	34·1
L21	Arderait	18½″ × 24″	2′ 4½″	4′ 0″	9′ 0″	23′ 3″	46′ 10½″	180	1184	137	1321	21	23,102	46·9	59·35	2855	325	36·45
E868	Arenuleux	17½″ × 23″	2′ 4½″	3′ 7¼″	8′ 0″	21′ 3½″	46′ 2″	180	976	113	1089	17·5	22,046	38	49·1	2530	256	34·1

Reference No. **L 300.**

Reference No. **E 903.**

Reference No. **L 21.**

Reference No. **E 868.**

2.8.0. Type

Locomotives with Tenders

3 ft. 6 in. Gau[ge]

Reference No. **L 14.**

Reference No.	Code Word.	Cylinders. Diam. × Stroke.	Wheels (Diam.). Front.	Wheels (Diam.). Coupled.	Wheel Base. Rigid.	Wheel Base. Engine.	Wheel Base. E. and T.	Boiler Working Pressure.	Heating Surfaces. Tubes.	Heating Surfaces. Firebox.	Heating Surfaces. Total.	Grate Area.	Tractive Force at 75 % B.P.	Engine Weight. Ad-hesive.	Engine Weight. Total.	Tender. Tank Capacity.	Tender. Fuel.	Tender. Weight Full.
								Lbs.	Sq. Ft.	Sq. Ft.	Sq. Ft.	Sq. Ft.	Lbs.	Tons.	Tons.	Gals.	Cub. Ft.	Tons.
L14	Ardeolis	$18\frac{1}{2}'' \times 24''$	$2' 4\frac{1}{2}''$	4′ 0″	14′ 6″	21′ 8″	$46' 11\frac{3}{4}''$	180	1355	106	1461	32	23,102	51·4	55·95	2855	325	36·45
E757	Arenosam	$15\frac{1}{2}'' \times 21''$	2′ 3″	3′ 0″	12′ 9″	20′ 3″	41′ 9″	160	776	86	862	15·75	16,840	31·25	35·5	2000	160	24·88

Reference No. **E 757.** Engine Tank Capacity 500 Gallons.

Tank Locomotives

3 ft. 6 in. Gauge

Reference No. E 758. 4.4.4. TYPE.

Reference No.	Code Word.	Cylinders.	Wheels (Diam.).			Wheel Base.		Boiler Working Pressure.	Heating Surfaces.			Grate Area.	Tractive Force at 75 % B.P.	Engine Weight.		Tank Capacity.	Fuel.
		Diam. × Stroke.	Front.	Coupled.	Hind.	Rigid.	Engine.		Tubes	Firebox.	Total.			Ad-hesive.	Total.		
								Lbs.	Sq. Ft.	Sq. Ft.	Sq. Ft.	Sq. Ft.	Lbs.	Tons.	Tons.	Gals.	Cub. Ft.
E758	Arenose	15½″ × 21″	2′ 3″	4′ 0″	2′ 3″	7′ 0″	29′ 6″	160	776	86	862	15·75	12,640	23·95	47	1600	96
E698	Arenghiera	10″ × 20″	—	3′ 2″	—	5′ 0″	5′ 0″	140	357	32	389	5·75	5,523	19·4	19·4	500	28
2703E	Argamasare	15″ × 22″	2′ 4″	4′ 1″	—	7′ 0″	18′ 1″	150	578	67	645	10	11,364	24	32·8	600	38

Reference No. E 698. 0.4.0. TYPE.

Reference No. 2703 E. 4.4.0. TYPE.

2.4.2. Type

Tank Locomotives

3 ft. 6 in. Gaug

Reference No. **L 284.**

Reference No. **4009 E.**

Reference No.	Code Word.	Cylinders.	Wheels (Diam.).			Wheel Base.		Boiler Working Pressure.	Heating Surfaces.			Grate Area.	Tractive Force at 75 % B.P.	Engine Weight.		Tank Capacity.	Fuel.
		Diam. × Stroke.	Front.	Coupled.	Hind.	Rigid.	Engine.		Tubes.	Firebox.	Total.			Adhesive.	Total.		
								Lbs.	Sq. Ft.	Sq. Ft.	Sq. Ft.	Sq. Ft.	Lbs.	Tons.	Tons.	Gals.	Cub. Ft.
L284	Arelad	14″ × 20″	3′ 1″	4′ 1″	3′ 1″	7′ 6″	19′ 6″	150	652	63	715	11·6	9,000	20·35	36·15	1000	45
4009E	Argemone	14″ × 20″	3′ 1″	4′ 4″	3′ 1″	7′ 6″	19′ 6″	140	652	63	715	11·6	7,915	19·1	36·5	1000	50
E1178	Aretinum	13″ × 18″	3′ 0″	4′ 6″	3′ 0″	6′ 0″	16′ 6″	140	535	60	595	11·25	5,914	17·95	33·95	1000	56
2765E	Argamaso	13″ × 18″	3′ 1″	4′ 0″	3′ 1″	6′ 0″	15′ 10″	140	446	49	495	8·5	6,654	18	29·37	700	60

Reference No. **E 1178.**

Reference No. **2765 E.**

D*

2.4.2. Type

Tank Locomotives

3 ft. 6 in. Gauge

Reference No. 3174 E.

Reference No.	Code Word.	Cylinders.	Wheels (Diam.).			Wheel Base.		Boiler Working Pressure.	Heating Surfaces.			Grate Area.	Tractive Force at 75 % B.P.	Engine Weight.		Tank Capacity.	Fuel.
		Diam. × Stroke.	Front.	Coupled.	Hind.	Rigid.	Engine.		Tubes.	Firebox.	Total.			Adhesive.	Total.		
								Lbs.	Sq. Ft.	Sq. Ft.	Sq. Ft.	Sq. Ft.	Lbs.	Tons.	Tons.	Gals.	Cub. Ft.
3174E	Arganello	$11'' \times 18''$	$2'\ 0\frac{3}{8}''$	$3'\ 9\frac{1}{8}''$	$2'\ 0\frac{3}{8}''$	$6'\ 6\frac{3}{4}''$	$19'\ 4\frac{1}{4}''$	142	362	38	400	7·5	5,154	11·75	20·7	400	35
E645	Arengaron	$13'' \times 18''$	3′ 3″	4′ 6″	2′ 6″	12′ 0″	17′ 9″	140	533	55	588	9	5,915	16	31·07	1100	60
E613	Arengamos	$9\frac{1}{2}'' \times 18''$	1′ 6″	3′ 0″	1′ 6″	5′ 0″	16′ 1″	130	360	32	392	7·25	4,388	10·5	17·97	300	48

Reference No. E 645.

Reference No. E 613.

0.6.0. Type

Tank Locomotives

3 ft. 6 in. Gauge

Reference No. L 64.

Reference No.	Code Word.	Cylinders.	Wheels (Diam.).	Wheel Base.		Boiler Working Pressure.	Heating Surfaces.			Grate Area.	Tractive Force at 75 % B.P.	Engine Weight.		Tank Capacity.	Fuel.
		Diam. × Stroke.	Coupled.	Rigid.	Engine.		Tubes.	Firebox.	Total.			Adhesive.	Total.		
						Lbs.	Sq. Ft.	Sq. Ft.	Sq. Ft.	Sq. Ft.	Lbs.	Tons.	Tons.	Gals.	Cub. Ft.
L64	Ardescis	16″ × 20″	3′ 3″	11′ 3″	11′ 3″	160	920	79	999	20·5	15,754	42·5	42·5	800	60
L240	Arefeceris	17″ × 22″	3′ 3″	10′ 0″	10′ 0″	160	809	72	881	16	19,563	40·3	40·3	800	48
L275	Arefies	15″ × 22″	3′ 0″	10′ 0″	10′ 0″	150	607	62	669	11·2	15,469	28	28	600	44

Reference No. L 240.

Reference No. L 275.

.6.0. Type

Tank Locomotives

3 ft. 6 in. Gauge

Reference No. **3324 E.**

Reference No. **E 1037.**

Reference No.	Code Word.	CYLINDERS. Diam. × Stroke.	WHEELS (Diam.). Coupled.	WHEEL BASE. Rigid.	WHEEL BASE. Engine.	Boiler Working Pressure.	HEATING SURFACES. Tubes.	HEATING SURFACES. Firebox.	HEATING SURFACES. Total.	Grate Area.	Tractive Force at 75 % B.P.	ENGINE WEIGHT. Adhesive.	ENGINE WEIGHT. Total.	Tank Capacity.	Fuel.
						Lbs.	Sq. Ft.	Sq. Ft.	Sq. Ft.	Sq. Ft.	Lbs.	Tons.	Tons.	Gals.	Cub. Ft.
3324E	ARGANTREE	15″ × 22″	4′ 0″	13′ 7″	13′ 7″	140	756	77	833	14	10,828	38·2	38·2	970	65
E1037	ARESTEIRO	15″ × 20″	4′ 0″	13′ 0″	13′ 0″	140	714	73	787	12·4	9,844	32·3	32·3	700	45
3263E	ARGANIAMO	14″ × 20″	3′ 9″	11′ 0″	11′ 0″	150	638	66	704	11·25	9,800	30·85	30·85	800	42
3420E	ARGAYANDO	14″ × 18″	3′ 0″	11′ 0″	11′ 0″	150	470	51	521	9·6	11,025	28·6	28·6	810	40
E1092	ARETALOGIA	13″ × 18″	3′ 0″	10′ 6″	10′ 6″	140	442	46	488	8	8,872	22·4	22·4	450	30
2419E	ARGALLERA	13″ × 18″	3′ 0″	10′ 6″	10′ 6″	140	446	48	494	8	8,872	23·77	23·77	450	35

Reference No. **3263 E.**

Reference No. **3420 E.**

Reference No. **E 1092.**

Reference No. **2419 E.**

0.6.0. Type

Tank Locomotives

3 ft. 6 in. Gauge

Reference No. **L 405.**

Reference No. **L 163.**

Reference No.	Code Word.	Cylinders.	Wheels (Diam.).	Wheel Base.		Boiler Working Pressure.	Heating Surfaces.			Grate Area.	Tractive Force at 75 % B.P.	Engine Weight.		Tank Capacity.	Fuel.
		Diam. × Stroke.	Coupled.	Rigid.	Engine.		Tubes.	Firebox.	Total.			Adhesive.	Total.		
						Lbs.	Sq. Ft.	Sq. Ft.	Sq. Ft.	Sq. Ft.	Lbs.	Tons.	Tons.	Gals.	Cub. Ft.
L405	Arencado	13″ × 18″	3′ 3½″	10′ 6″	10′ 6″	160	475	56	531	9·2	9,241	28·25	28·25	700	35
L163	Ardurous	12¼″ × 18″	3′ 0″	10′ 6″	10′ 6″	150	446	40	486	9	8,441	21·2	21·2	450	27
E622	Arengaras	10½″ × 18″	3′ 0½″	10′ 6″	10′ 6″	140	446	41	487	9·3	5,690	20·6	20·6	450	29
E611	Arengais	9″ × 14″	2′ 4″	9′ 0″	9′ 0″	130	220	31	251	5·5	3,924	15·27	15·27	260	70

Reference No. **E 622.**

Reference No. **E 611.**

0.6.2. Type

Tank Locomotives

3 ft. 6 in. Gauge

Reference No. **L 108.**

Reference No. **L 2.**

Reference No.	Code Word.	Cylinders.	Wheels (Diam.).		Wheel Base.		Boiler Working Pressure.	Heating Surfaces.			Grate Area.	Tractive Force at 75 % B.P.	Engine Weight.		Tank Capacity.	Fuel.
		Diam. × Stroke.	Coupled.	Hind.	Rigid.	Engine.		Tubes.	Firebox.	Total.			Ad-hesive.	Total.		
							Lbs.	Sq. Ft.	Sq. Ft.	Sq. Ft.	Sq. Ft.	Lbs.	Tons.	Tons.	Gals.	Cub. Ft.
L108	Ardesselo	16″ × 24″	4′ 1″	3′ 2″	12′ 6″	19′ 9″	160	906	94	1000	14·5	15,046	40·2	49·5	1716	76
L2	Ardenza	16″ × 24″	4′ 0″	3′ 1″	12′ 6″	19′ 9″	140	906	92	998	14·3	13,440	39·15	48·5	1700	65
L431	Arendskop	13″ × 18″	3′ 4½″	2′ 7½″	12′ 0″	17′ 9″	180	533	55	588	9	10,140	27·75	35·02	1100	60
L271	Arefecit	13″ × 20″	3′ 1″	2′ 2″	9′ 3″	15′ 6″	150	545	52	597	10	10,277	23·65	29·8	1000	67

Reference No. **L 431.**

Reference No. **L 271.**

Tank Locomotives

3 ft. 6 in. Gauge

Reference No. **2317 E.** **4.6.0. TYPE.**

Reference No. **3182 E.** **0.6.4. TYPE.**

Reference No.	Code Word.	Cylinders.	Wheels (Diam.).			Wheel Base.		Boiler Working Pressure.	Heating Surfaces.			Grate Area.	Tractive Force at 75 % B.P.	Engine Weight.		Tank Capacity.	Fuel.
		Diam. × Stroke.	Front.	Coupled.	Hind.	Rigid.	Engine.		Tubes.	Firebox.	Total.			Adhesive.	Total.		
								Lbs.	Sq. Ft.	Sq. Ft.	Sq. Ft.	Sq. Ft.	Lbs.	Tons.	Tons.	Gals.	Cub. Ft.
2317E	Argallas	14″ × 20″	2′ 2½″	3′ 9″	—	9′ 9″	18′ 9″	150	700	63	763	12	9,800	28·05	34·35	780	40
3182E	Arganero	16″ × 20″	—	3′ 3″	2′ 3″	8′ 0″	19′ 10½″	150	918	85	1003	17	14,769	33·1	45·4	1300	76
L33	Ardescendo	14½″ × 20″	2′ 3″	3′ 3″	—	10′ 3″	16′ 9″	150	615	76	691	12·6	12,130	33	38	1100	58
E627	Arengaria	13″ × 18″	—	3′ 1″	1′ 10½″	6′ 7″	15′ 4″	130	466	49	515	9·5	8,015	18·45	24·75	500	45

Reference No. **L 33.** **2.6.0. TYPE.**

Reference No. **E 627.** **0.6.4. TYPE.**

Tank Locomotives

3 ft. 6 in. Gauge

Reference No. **E 878.** **4.6.4. TYPE.**

Reference No. **2179 E.** **2.6.2. TYPE.**

Reference No.	Code Word.	Cylinders.	Wheels (Diam.).			Wheel Base.		Boiler Working Pressure.	Heating Surfaces.			Grate Area.	Tractive Force at 75 % B.P.	Engine Weight.		Tank Capacity.	Fuel.
		Diam. × Stroke.	Front.	Coupled.	Hind.	Rigid.	Engine.		Tubes.	Firebox.	Total.			Ad-hesive.	Total.		
								Lbs.	Sq. Ft.	Sq. Ft.	Sq. Ft.	Sq. Ft.	Lbs.	Tons.	Tons.	Gals.	Cub. Ft.
E878	Areolaire	15″ × 22″	2′ 1¾″	3′ 2″	2′ 1¾″	7′ 9″	25′ 7¼″	175	803	70	873	12·7	17,097	24·5	43·1	1000	90
2179E	Argadillos	15″ × 20″	2′ 3″	3′ 3″	2′ 3″	7′ 4″	19′ 6″	150	772	78	850	14·5	12,980	27·87	37·43	700	36
L313	Arelaras	12″ × 18″	2′ 0″	3′ 0″	2′ 0″	8′ 6″	20′ 3″	150	465	49	514	9·5	8,100	18·3	26·75	750	100
3172E	Arganeles	11″ × 18″	2′ 0⅜″	3′ 0″	2′ 0⅜″	8′ 2⅜″	20′ 8″	142	413	38	451	7·5	6,443	14·55	22·2	450	35

Reference No. **L 313.** **2.6.2. TYPE.**

Reference No. **3172 E.** **2.6.2. TYPE.**

Tank Locomotives

3 ft. 6 in. Gauge

Reference No. L 12. 4.8.2. TYPE.

Reference No.	Code Word.	Cylinders.	Wheels (Diam.).			Wheel Base.		Boiler Working Pressure.	Heating Surfaces.			Grate Area.	Tractive Force at 75 % B.P.	Engine Weight.		Tank Capacity.	Fuel.
		Diam. × Stroke.	Front.	Coupled.	Hind.	Rigid.	Engine.		Tubes.	Firebox.	Total.			Adhesive.	Total.		
								Lbs.	Sq. Ft.	Sq. Ft.	Sq. Ft.	Sq. Ft.	Lbs.	Tons.	Tons.	Gals.	Cub. Ft.
L12	Ardeolarum	18″ × 22″	2′ 1¾″	3′ 6″	2′ 1¾″	7′ 10″	26′ 9½″	175	1098	125	1223	19	22,275	42·35	62·5	1500	100
3317E	Argantidae	17″ × 21″	2′ 1¾″	3′ 3″	2′ 1¾″	7′ 4″	24′ 9″	160	888	90	978	15·7	18,674	29·1	48·2	1200	90
E858	Arenularum	17″ × 21″	2′ 1″	3′ 2″	2′ 1″	11′ 3″	28′ 0″	160	919	93	1012	16·7	19,134	33·35	52·0	2000	114

Reference No. 3317 E. 4.8.2. TYPE

Reference No. E 858. 2.8.4. TYPE.

Tank Locomotives

3 ft. 6 in. Gauge

Reference No. **L 356.** **4.6.2. TYPE.**

Reference No.	Code Word.	Cylinders.	Wheels (Diam.).			Wheel Base.		Boiler Working Pressure.	Heating Surfaces.			Grate Area.	Tractive Force at 75 % B.P.	Engine Weight.		Tank Capacity.	Fuel.
		Diam. × Stroke.	Front.	Coupled.	Hind.	Rigid.	Engine.		Tubes.	Firebox.	Total.			Adhesive.	Total.		
								Lbs.	Sq. Ft.	Sq. Ft.	Sq. Ft.	Sq. Ft.	Lbs.	Tons.	Tons.	Gals.	Cub. Ft.
L356	Arenaceo	16″ × 24″	2′ 7½″	4′ 0″	2′ 7½″	12′ 3″	28′ 7½″	180	973	107	1080	16·5	17,280	33·7	57·15	1400	60
3835E	Argemata	19″ × 27″	2′ 1½″	3′ 9″	2′ 1½″	8′ 4″	30′ 6″	175	1359	134	1493	21	28,428	53·2	70·9	1720	160
3653E	Argelino	17″ × 23″	2′ 4½″	4′ 6″	2′ 4½″	9′ 0″	28′ 7½″	160	893	93	986	26	14,771	33·57	53·9	1300	90

Reference No. **3835 E.** **4.10.2. TYPE.**

Reference No. **3653 E.** **4.6.2. TYPE.**

Locomotives for the Metre Gauge

0.6.6.0. Type "Mallet" Articulated Compound Locomotives with Tenders Metre Gauge

Reference No. **L 384.**

Reference No.	Code Word.	Cylinders. Diam. × Stroke.	Wheels (Diam.). Coupled.	Wheel Base. Rigid.	Wheel Base. Engine.	Wheel Base. E. and T.	Boiler Working Pressure.	Heating Surfaces. Tubes.	Heating Surfaces. Firebox.	Heating Surfaces. Total.	Grate Area.	Tractive Force at 60 % B.P.	Engine Weight. Adhesive.	Engine Weight. Total.	Tender. Tank Capacity.	Tender. Fuel.	Tender. Weight Full.
							Lbs.	Sq. Ft.	Sq. Ft.	Sq. Ft	Sq. Ft.	Lbs.	Tons.	Tons.	Gals.	Cub. Ft.	Tons.
L384	Arenassent	$15\frac{1}{2}''$ & $24\frac{1}{4}'' \times 20''$	3′ 3″	8′ 3″	24′ 3″	48′ 7″	180	1398	115	1513	33	26,612	58·22	58·22	2000	270	31·32
L350	Arenaceior	$18''$ & $28'' \times 24''$	3′ 9″	8′ 11″	26′ 4″	50′ 8″	180	2070	135	2205	40	37,325	81·9	81·9	3080	202	35·25
L416	Arencaste	$17''$ & $26\frac{1}{2}'' \times 24''$	3′ 9″	8′ 11″	26′ 4″	50′ 8″	180	1863	122	1985	36	33,293	74·4	74·4	3080	202	35·25
L418	Arendalite	$15\frac{1}{2}''$ & $24\frac{1}{4}'' \times 20''$	3′ 3″	8′ 3″	24′ 3″	43′ 10″	180	1398	115	1513	33	26,612	58·07	58·07	2000	320	24·65

Reference No. **L 418.**

Reference No. **L 416.**

Reference No. **L 350.**

4.4.0. Type

Locomotives with Tenders

Metre Gauge

Reference No. **L 153.**

Reference No.	Code Word.	Cylinders.	Wheels (Diam.).		Wheel Base.			Boiler Working Pressure.	Heating Surfaces.			Grate Area.	Tractive Force at 75 % B.P.	Engine Weight.		Tender.		
		Diam. × Stroke.	Front.	Coupled.	Rigid.	Engine.	E. and T.		Tubes.	Firebox.	Total.			Adhesive.	Total.	Tank Capacity.	Fuel.	Weight Full.
								Lbs.	Sq. Ft.	Sq. Ft.	Sq. Ft.	Sq. Ft.	Lbs.	Tons.	Tons.	Gals.	Cub. Ft.	Tons.
L153	Arduously	16″ × 20″	2′ 7″	4′ 8″	8′ 6″	20′ 6″	41′ 6″	160	899	106	1005	15	10,970	19·45	34	2500	169	30·8
E764	Arenosorum	16″ × 22″	2′ 6″	4′ 9″	9′ 9″	23′ 1″	43′ 5⅝″	170	727	81	808	16·4	12,600	21·6	33·45	2000	350	25·75
E938	Areopagist	15″ & 21½″ × 22″	2′ 6′	4′ 6″	7′ 0″	18′ 11½″	39′ 3⅛″	175	742	76	818	13·5	9,625	22·1	32·58	1760	100	20

Tractive Force **E 938** taken at 60% B.P.

Reference No. **E 764.**

Reference No. **E 938.** 2 Cylinder "Compound."

4.4.0. Type

Locomotives with Tenders

Metre Gauge

Reference No. **L 149.**

Reference No. **E 601.**

Reference No.	Code Word.	Cylinders.	Wheels (Diam.).		Wheel Base.			Boiler Working Pressure.	Heating Surfaces.			Grate Area.	Tractive Force at 75 % B.P.	Engine Weight.		Tender.		
		Diam. × Stroke.	Front.	Coupled.	Rigid.	Engine.	E. and T.		Tubes.	Firebox.	Total.			Adhesive.	Total.	Tank Capacity.	Fuel.	Weight Full.
								Lbs.	Sq. Ft.	Sq. Ft.	Sq. Ft.	Sq. Ft.	Lbs.	Tons.	Tons.	Gals.	Cub. Ft.	Tons.
L149	Arduissimo	14″ × 20″	2′ 1⅜″	4′ 5″	6′ 0″	15′ 5″	36′ 3⅞″	140	570	59	629	12	7,765	16·07	23·25	2000	160	22·52
E601	Arengad	14″ × 20″	2′ 4½″	4′ 5″	6′ 0″	15′ 2″	30′ 3⅛″	140	496	52	548	10·5	7,765	16·4	23·87	1000	250	14
E1095	Aretalogos	14″ × 20″	2′ 3″	4′ 3″	7′ 0″	18′ 10″	33′ 3″	140	608	66	674	12·25	8,070	15·6	25·2	1090	260	14
E957	Arepas	13″ × 16″	2′ 2″	3′ 7½″	7′ 6″	17′ 11″	36′ 8½″	150	528	56	584	9·5	6,990	13·85	22·05	1200	33	16·5

Reference No. **E 1095.**

Reference No. **E 957.**

Locomotives with Tenders

Metre Gauge

Reference No. **3312 E.** **4.4.0. TYPE.**

Reference No. **E 708.** **4.4.0. TYPE.**
Engine, Tank Capacity 360 Gallons.

Reference No. **L 205.** **4.4.2. TYPE.**

Reference No. **L 230.** **2.4.2. TYPE.**

Reference No.	Code Word.	Cylinders.	Wheels (Diam.).			Wheel Base.			Boiler Working Pressure.	Heating Surfaces.			Grate Area.	Tractive Force at 75 % B.P.	Engine Weight.		Tender.		
		Diam. × Stroke.	Front.	Coupled.	Hind.	Rigid.	Engine.	E. and T.		Tubes.	Firebox.	Total.			Adhesive.	Total.	Tank Capacity.	Fuel.	Weight Full.
									Lbs.	Sq. Ft.	Sq. Ft.	Sq. Ft.	Sq. Ft.	Lbs.	Tons.	Tons.	Gals.	Cub. Ft.	Tons.
3312E	ARGANIATE	14″ × 20″	2′ 1″	3′ 6″	—	6′ 3″	17′ 8″	33′ 5″	140	574	64	638	12·7	9,800	16·05	23·17	1500	90	17·4
E708	ARENIFERE	12″ × 18″	1′ 11″	3′ 3″	—	7′ 0″	17′ 2″	31′ 3¾″	140	444	59	503	9	6,978	14·86	22·56	1000	180	12·65
L205	ARECISTEIS	17″ × 24″	2′ 7″	4′ 9″	2′ 10″	5′ 3″	24′ 4″	47′ 7″	200	981	97	1078	23·7	18,252	26	50	3300	360	42·65
L230	AREFECERAT	13″ × 20″	2′ 4½″	3′ 6½″	2′ 4½″	4′ 10″	16′ 6″	35′ 4″	160	527	66	593	13	9,543	13·8	25·8	2000	250	21·2
E719	ARENIVAGAM	13″ × 20″	2′ 4″	3′ 6″	—	10′ 3″	10′ 3″	29′ 6″	140	496	54	550	9·6	8,450	14·15	20·2	2000	250	20·9

Reference No. **E 719.** **2.4.0. TYPE.**

Locomotives with Tenders

Metre Gauge

Reference No. **L 287.** **2.6.0. TYPE.**

Reference No.	Code Word.	Cylinders.	Wheels (Diam.).		Wheel Base.			Boiler Working Pressure.	Heating Surfaces.			Grate Area.	Tractive Force at 75 % B.P.	Engine Weight.		Tender.		
		Diam. × Stroke.	Front.	Coupled.	Rigid.	Engine.	E. and T.		Tubes.	Firebox.	Total.			Adhesive.	Total.	Tank Capacity.	Fuel.	Weight Full.
								Lbs.	Sq. Ft.	Sq. Ft.	Sq. Ft.	Sq. Ft.	Lbs.	Tons.	Tons.	Gals.	Cub. Ft.	Tons.
L287	Arelamos	16″ × 20″	2′ 7″	3′ 6″	10′ 6″	18′ 6″	41′ 5⅞″	160	903	105	1008	15	14,628	29·87	35·02	2000	160	27·37
E797	Arentes	14½″ × 20″	—	3′ 6½″	11′ 0″	11′ 0″	28′ 7½″	160	670	75	745	12·8	11,858	30·1	30·1	1500	155	18·7
L392	Arenation	14″ × 20″	—	3′ 7″	11′ 0″	11′ 0″	31′ 2½″	160	583	62	645	12·5	10,940	23·57	23·57	2000	350	22·97

Reference No. **E 797.** **0.6.0. TYPE.**

Reference No. **L 392.** **0.6.0. TYPE.**

F*

Locomotives with Tenders

Metre Gauge

Reference No. **L 26.** **0.6.0. TYPE.**

Reference No. **L 204.** **4.6.2. TYPE.**

Reference No.	Code Word.	Cylinders.	Wheels (Diam.).			Wheel Base.			Boiler Working Pressure.	Heating Surfaces.			Grate Area.	Tractive Force at 75 % B.P.	Engine Weight.		Tender.		
		Diam. × Stroke.	Front.	Coupled.	Hind.	Rigid.	Engine.	E. and T.		Tubes.	Firebox.	Total.			Ad-hesive.	Total.	Tank Capacity.	Fuel.	Weight Full.
									Lbs.	Sq. Ft.	Sq. Ft.	Sq. Ft.	Sq. Ft.	Lbs.	Tons.	Tons.	Gals.	Cub. Ft.	Tons.
L26	Arderions	14″ × 20″	—	3′ 6½″	—	11′ 6″	11′ 6″	29′ 9″	160	587	68	655	12·5	11,068	23	23	1500	260	18·15
L204	Arecineas	18″ × 24″	2′ 7″	4′ 0″	2′ 10″	9′ 0″	27′ 4″	50′ 7″	200	1107	97	1204	23·7	24,300	40	54·8	3300	360	42·65
L334	Arelasen	16″ × 22″	2′ 7½″	4′ 0″	—	11′ 3″	20′ 9″	42′ 8″	170	910	95·5	1005·5	15·5	14,960	27·6	36·1	2500	213	29 2
L173	Arecera	18″ × 22″	2′ 7″	4′ 6″	2′ 7″	9′ 6″	28′ 4″	49′ 1″	180	1461	102	1563	23	17,820	36·1	54·25	3000	240	33·7

Reference No. **L 334.** **4.6.0. TYPE.**

Reference No. **L 173.** **4.6.2. TYPE.**

4.6.0. Type

Locomotives with Tenders

Metre Gauge

Reference No. **L 255.**

Reference No.	Code Word.	Cylinders.	Wheels (Diam.).		Wheel Base.			Boiler Working Pressure.	Heating Surfaces.			Grate Area.	Tractive Force at 75 % B.P.	Engine Weight.		Tender.		
		Diam. × Stroke.	Front.	Coupled.	Rigid.	Engine.	E. and T.		Tubes.	Firebox.	Total.			Ad-hesive.	Total.	Tank Capacity.	Fuel.	Weight Full.
								Lbs.	Sq. Ft.	Sq. Ft.	Sq. Ft.	Sq. Ft.	Lbs.	Tons.	Tons.	Gals.	Cub. Ft.	Tons.
L255	Arefecimus	15½″ × 22″	2′ 4½″	4′ 9″	12′ 0″	21′ 1½″	42′ 2¼″	180	954	108	1062	16	12,518	26·1	33·5	2000	180	23
L116	Ardour	15½″ × 22″	2′ 4½″	4′ 9″	12′ 0″	21′ 1½″	43′ 1¾″	180	954	108	1062	16	12,518	26·85	34·65	1850	300	24 5

Reference No. **L 116.**

4.6.0. Type

Locomotives with Tenders

Metre Gauge

Reference No. **L 254.**

Reference No.	Code Word.	Cylinders.	Wheels (Diam.).		Wheel Base.			Boiler Working Pressure.	Heating Surfaces.			Grate Area.	Tractive Force at 75 % B.P.	Engine Weight.		Tender.		
		Diam. × Stroke.	Front.	Coupled.	Rigid.	Engine.	E. and T.		Tubes.	Firebox.	Total.			Adhesive.	Total.	Tank Capacity.	Fuel.	Weight Full.
								Lbs.	Sq. Ft.	Sq. Ft.	Sq. Ft.	Sq. Ft.	Lbs.	Tons.	Tons.	Gals.	Cub. Ft.	Tons.
L254	Arefecero	15″ × 22″	2′ 4½″	4′ 0″	12′ 0″	21′ 1″	42′ 1¼″	180	954	108	1062	16	13,921	26	33·4	2000	180	23
L279	Areignol	15″ × 22″	2′ 4½″	4′ 0″	12′ 0″	21′ 1″	42′ 1¾″	180	954	108	1062	16	13,921	26·93	34·86	2000	180	23·35

Reference No. **L 279.**

4.6.0. Type

Locomotives with Tenders

Metre Gauge

Reference No. **E 874.**

Reference No.	Code Word.	• Cylinders.	Wheels (Diam.).		Wheel Base.			Boiler Working Pressure.	Heating Surfaces.			Grate Area.	Tractive Force at 75 % B.P.	Engine Weight.		Tender.		
		Diam. × Stroke.	Front.	Coupled.	Rigid.	Engine.	E. and T.		Tubes.	Firebox.	Total.			Ad-hesive.	Total.	Tank Capacity.	Fuel.	Weight Full.
								Lbs.	Sq. Ft.	Sq. Ft.	Sq. Ft.	Sq. Ft.	Lbs.	Tons.	Tons.	Gals.	Cub. Ft.	Tons.
E874	Arenzata	15″ × 22″	2′ 4½″	5′ 0″	12′ 0″	21′ 1½″	41′ 8¾″	180	907	96	1003	15	11,138	24·75	32·5	2000	180	22·95
E887	Areolar	15″ × 22″	2′ 4½″	4′ 0″	12′ 0″	21′ 1½″	41′ 8¾″	180	907	96	1003	15	13,922	24·77	32·1	2000	180	22·95
E1189	Arfardes	14½″ × 20″	2′ 4½″	4′ 0″	10′ 8″	19′ 8½″	40′ 8¾″	180	805	92	897	15	11,826	23·25	30·6	1800	135	21·3

Reference No. **E 887.**

Reference No. **E 1189.**

4.6.0. Type

Locomotives with Tenders

Metre Gauge

Reference No. **L 282.**

Reference No. **L 387.**

Reference No.	Code Word.	Cylinders.	Wheels (Diam.).		Wheel Base.			Boiler Working Pressure.	Heating Surfaces.			Grate Area.	Tractive Force at 75 % B.P.	Engine Weight.		Tender.		
		Diam. × Stroke.	Front.	Coupled.	Rigid.	Engine.	E. and T.		Tubes.	Firebox.	Total.			Ad-hesive.	Total.	Tank Capacity.	Fuel.	Weight Full.
								Lbs.	Sq. Ft.	Sq. Ft.	Sq. Ft.	Sq. Ft.	Lbs.	Tons.	Tons.	Gals.	Cub. Ft.	Tons.
L282	Arelaban	15¼″ × 18″	2′ 2″	3′ 4″	9′ 0″	17′ 5″	37′ 6″	140	698	66	764	12·5	10,988	22·5	28·3	1200	180	19·25
L387	Arenatae	15″ × 22″	2′ 6″	4′ 4″	9′ 6″	18′ 11″	41′ 5⅛″	175	886	86	972	16	12,493	25·05	34·45	1500	200	20·9
E871	Arenvisch	14½″ × 20″	2′ 3½″	4′ 3½″	6′ 9″	20′ 6″	38′ 6″	150	662	70	732	13	9,170	22·05	29·85	1770	240	20·15
3220E	Arganetti	14″ × 20″	1′ 11″	3′ 3″	8′ 9″	17′ 3½″	33′ 3¾″	140	616	67	683	12	10,554	19·95	26·3	1000	250	16·95
E927	Areometric	14″ × 18″	2′ 2″	3′ 4″	8′ 6″	16′ 8″	37′ 8½″	140	611	59	670	11·87	9,261	18·8	23·9	1200	135	16·5
E969	Arepenne	14″ × 18″	2′ 2″	3′ 4″	8′ 6″	16′ 8″	35′ 6½″	140	611	59	670	11·9	9,261	19·15	24·1	1100	135	16·5

Reference No. **E 871.**

Reference No. **3220 E.**

Reference No. **E 927.**

Reference No. **E 969.**

2.8.0. Type

Locomotives with Tenders

Metre Gauge

Reference No. **L 228.**

Reference No.	Code Word.	Cylinders.	Wheels (Diam.).		Wheel Base.			Boiler Working Pressure.	Heating Surfaces.			Grate Area.	Tractive Force at 75 % B.P.	Engine Weight.		Tender.		
		Diam. × Stroke.	Front.	Coupled.	Rigid.	Engine.	E. and T.		Tubes.	Firebox.	Total.			Adhesive.	Total.	Tank Capacity.	Fuel.	Weight Full.
								Lbs.	Sq. Ft.	Sq. Ft.	Sq. Ft.	Sq. Ft.	Lbs.	Tons.	Tons.	Gals.	Cub. Ft.	Tons.
L228	Arefatto	15″ × 18″	2′ 2″	3′ 1″	11′ 6″	18′ 0″	41′ 0$\frac{7}{8}$″	160	737	96	833	14	13,135	29·2	33·2	2000	160	27·3
E939	Areopagus	16″ & 23″ × 24″	2′ 3″	3′ 6″	12′ 7″	19′ 2″	40′ 3″	175	845	92	937	15	15,360	33·15	37·4	1980	90	21·35
E1208	Argadijo	15″ × 18″	2′ 2″	3′ 1″	11′ 6″	17′ 8″	39′ 1″	160	732	86	818	14·33	13,135	25·3	29·25	1300	220	19·65

Tractive Force **E 939** taken at 60 % B.P.

Reference No. **E 939.** 2-Cylinder Compound.

Reference No. **E 1208.**

Locomotives with Tenders

Metre Gauge

Reference No. **L432.** **2.8.2. TYPE.**

Reference No.	Code Word.	Cylinders.	Wheels (Diam.).			Wheel Base.			Boiler Working Pressure.	Heating Surfaces.			Grate Area.	Tractive Force at 75 % B.P.	Engine Weight.		Tender.		
		Diam. × Stroke.	Front.	Coupled.	Hind.	Rigid.	Engine.	E. and T.		Tubes.	Firebox.	Total.			Ad-hesive.	Total.	Tank Capacity.	Fuel.	Weight Full.
									Lbs.	Sq. Ft.	Sq. Ft.	Sq. Ft.	Sq. Ft.	Lbs.	Tons.	Tons.	Gals.	Cub. Ft.	Tons.
L432	Arendsneus	17″ × 22$\frac{1}{16}$″	2′ 6$\frac{3}{4}$″	3′ 6″	2′ 6$\frac{3}{4}$″	11′ 9$\frac{3}{4}$″	26′ 2″	47′ 11$\frac{3}{4}$″	176·4	1765	108	1873	27	20,084	40·65	57·95	3300	265	34·9
L178	Arecereis	19″ × 24″	2′ 4$\frac{1}{2}$″	3′ 9″	—	8′ 8″	23′ 0″	49′ 2″	180	1644	122	1766	31	25,992	53	63·2	3080	202	35·25

Reference No. **L178.** **4.8.0. TYPE.**

4.8.0. Type — **Locomotives with Tenders** — **Metre Gauge**

Reference No. **L 381.** 2-Cylinder Compound.

Reference No.	Code Word.	Cylinders.	Wheels (Diam.).		Wheel Base.			Boiler Working Pressure.	Heating Surfaces.			Grate Area.	Tractive Force at 75 % B.P.	Engine Weight.		Tender.		
		Diam. × Stroke.	Front.	Coupled.	Rigid.	Engine.	E. and T.		Tubes.	Firebox.	Total.			Ad-hesive.	Total.	Tank Capacity.	Fuel.	Weight Full.
								Lbs.	Sq. Ft.	Sq. Ft.	Sq. Ft.	Sq. Ft.	Lbs.	Tons.	Tons.	Gals.	Cub. Ft.	Tons.
L381	Arenarius	18″ & 26″ × 22″	2′ 7″	3′ 6″	8′ 0″	22′ 8″	48′ 0″	180	1510	112	1622	27·75	18,329	42·5	55·05	3000	180	34·27
L203	Arecieron	18″ × 22″	2′ 7″	3′ 6″	8′ 0″	22′ 8″	46′ 8½″	180	1510	112	1622	28	22,913	42·65	54·7	3000	240	33·7
L118	Ardrigh	18″ × 22″	2′ 7″	3′ 6″	7′ 11″	21′ 7½″	41′ 6″	160	1230	104	1334	25	20·366	35·25	46·2	2000	169	25·3

Tractive Force **L 381** taken at 60 % B.P.

Reference No. **L 203.**

Reference No. **L 118.**

.8.0. Type

Locomotives with Tenders

Metre Gauge

Reference No. **L 208.**

Reference No.	Code Word.	Cylinders.	Wheels (Diam.).		Wheel Base.			Boiler Working Pressure.	Heating Surfaces.			Grate Area.	Tractive Force at 75 % B.P.	Engine Weight.		Tender.		
		Diam. × Stroke.	Front.	Coupled.	Rigid.	Engine.	E. and T.		Tubes.	Firebox.	Total.			Adhesive.	Total.	Tank Capacity.	Fuel.	Weight Full.
								Lbs.	Sq. Ft.	Sq. Ft.	Sq. Ft.	Sq. Ft.	Lbs.	Tons.	Tons.	Gals.	Cub. Ft.	Tons.
L164	Areasneak	16″ × 22″	2′ 4½″	3′ 7″	8′ 0″	21′ 3″	46′ 3″	180	1166	126	1292	17·5	17,682	32·15	40·05	2000	135	25
L208	Arefaccao	16″ × 22″	2′ 4½″	3′ 7″	12′ 0″	20′ 6″	42′ 3¼″	180	1166	126	1292	17·5	17,682	34	41	1600	450	22·52

Reference No. **L 164.**

Tank Locomotives

Metre Gaug

Reference No. **E 614.** **TYPE 0.4.0.**

Reference No. **E 707.** **TYPE 2.4.2.**

Reference No.	Code Word.	Cylinders.	Wheels (Diam.).			Wheel Base.		Boiler Working Pressure.	Heating Surfaces.			Grate Area.	Tractive Force at 75 % B.P.	Engine Weight.		Tank Capacity.	Fuel.
		Diam. × Stroke.	Front.	Coupled.	Hind.	Rigid.	Engine.		Tubes.	Firebox.	Total.			Ad-hesive.	Total.		
								Lbs.	Sq. Ft.	Sq. Ft.	Sq. Ft.	Sq. Ft.	Lbs.	Tons.	Tons.	Gals.	Cub. Ft.
E614	Arengando	$12\frac{1}{4}'' \times 18''$	—	3′ 0″	—	6′ 3″	6′ 3″	145	355	41	396	6·3	8,156	16·38	16·38	300	18
E707	Arenicolid	12″ × 18″	2′ 6″	3′ 6″	2′ 6″	6′ 6″	16′ 4″	140	445	54	499	8	6,480	13·15	25·1	600	60
3044E	Arganano	13″ × 20″	2′ 1″	3′ 6″	—	6′ 6″	12′ 8″	140	488	46	534	9·4	8,450	19·35	23·85	500	40
E1158	Aretichero	11″ × 18″	2′ 6″	3′ 6″	—	6′ 2″	11′ 4″	150	361	41	402	6·9	5,831	14	19·35	400	22

Reference No. **3044 E.** **TYPE 2.4.0.**

Reference No. **E 1158.** **TYPE 2.4.0.**

4.4.0. Type

Tank Locomotives

Metre Gauge

Reference No. **4345 E.**

Reference No. **3338 E.**

Reference No. **E 949.**

Reference No.	Code Word.	Cylinders.	Wheels (Diam.).		Wheel Base.		Boiler Working Pressure.	Heating Surfaces.			Grate Area.	Tractive Force at 75 % B.P.	Engine Weight.		Tank Capacity.	Fuel.
		Diam. × Stroke.	Front.	Coupled.	Rigid.	Engine.		Tubes.	Firebox.	Total.			Adhesive.	Total.		
							Lbs.	Sq. Ft.	Sq. Ft.	Sq. Ft.	Sq. Ft.	Lbs.	Tons.	Tons.	Gals.	Cub. Ft.
4345E	Argennorum	15½″ × 22″	2′ 3″	4′ 3½″	7′ 6″	19′ 3″	150	699	74	773	12	11,546	25·1	34·55	600	49
3338E	Argasidae	12″ × 18″	2′ 3″	3′ 6″	5′ 0″	15′ 3″	140	520	47	567	9·6	6,480	13·25	23·85	500	35
E949	Areostyle	14″ × 20″	2′ 3″	4′ 0″	6′ 8″	18′ 4″	140	520	56	576	11	8,575	19·5	26·1	600	33

Tank Locomotives

Metre Gauge

Reference No. **L 181.** **4.4.4. TYPE.**

Reference No. **3621 E.** **4.4.2. TYPE.**

Reference No.	Code Word.	Cylinders.	Wheels (Diam.).			Wheel Base.		Boiler Working Pressure.	Heating Surfaces.			Grate Area.	Tractive Force at 75 % B.P.	Engine Weight.		Tank Capacity.	Fuel.
		Diam. × Stroke.	Front.	Coupled.	Hind.	Rigid.	Engine.		Tubes.	Firebox.	Total.			Ad-hesive.	Total.		
								Lbs.	Sq. Ft.	Sq. Ft.	Sq. Ft.	Sq. Ft.	Lbs.	Tons.	Tons.	Gals.	Cub. Ft.
L181	Arecian	14″ × 20″	2′ 4½″	4′ 5″	2′ 4½″	6′ 7″	26′ 2″	150	570	59	629	12	8,320	15·5	37·45	960	87
3621E	Argayaria	12″ × 18″	2′ 0″	3′ 6″	2′ 0″	6′ 0″	21′ 6″	130	520	47	567	9·6	6,017	12	27	500	120
L368	Arenalillo	14¼″ × 20″	—	3′ 0″	2′ 2″	7′ 5″	14′ 11″	176	720	65	785	10	14,891	28	34·25	880	56
L172	Arecanut	16″ × 20″	—	3′ 9″	2′ 7″	12′ 0″	19′ 0″	180	861	93	954	13	15,360	39·08	47·83	1200	90

Reference No. **L 368.** **0.6.2. TYPE.**

Reference No. **L 172.** **0.6.2. TYPE.**

Tank Locomotives

Metre Gauge

Reference No. **E 1030.** **4.6.0. TYPE.**

Reference No. **3156 E.** **4.6.0. TYPE.**

Reference No. **E 917.** **0.6.0. TYPE.**

Reference No.	Code Word.	Cylinders. Diam. × Stroke.	Wheels (Diam.). Front.	Coupled.	Hind.	Wheel Base. Rigid.	Engine.	Boiler Working Pressure.	Heating Surfaces. Tubes.	Firebox.	Total.	Grate Area.	Tractive Force at 75 % B.P.	Engine Weight. Ad-hesive.	Total.	Tank Capacity.	Fuel.
								Lbs.	Sq. Ft.	Sq. Ft.	Sq. Ft.	Sq. Ft.	Lbs.	Tons.	Tons.	Gals.	Cub. Ft.
E1030	Areranhas	12″ × 18″	2′ 2″	3′ 0″	—	4′ 6″	15′ 10″	160	503	47	550	8·5	8,640	20·9	25·6	500	33
3156E	Arganaste	14″ × 20″	2′ 3″	3′ 3″	—	9′ 6″	18′ 9″	150	680	62	742	10·7	11,307	27·25	34	700	40
E917	Areometers	13″ × 20″	—	3′ 1″	—	10′ 0″	10′ 0″	150	524	47	571	9·75	10,277	23·5	23·5	400	33
3170E	Arganeis	14″ × 20″	2′ 0″	3′ 6″	2′ 0″	5′ 6″	24′ 0″	150	574	62	636	12·7	10,500	23·6	34·55	900	88
E1040	Arestil	14½″ × 18″	2′ 2″	3′ 6″	2′ 2″	9′ 6″	21′ 6″	140	629	65	694	12·5	9,460	23	33·7	675	80

Reference No. **3170 E.** **2.6.2. TYPE.**

Reference No. **E 1040.** **2.6.2. TYPE.**

2.6.2. Type

Tank Locomotives

Metre Gauge

Reference No. **L 256.**

Reference No.	Code Word.	Cylinders. Diam. × Stroke.	Wheels (Diam.). Front.	Coupled.	Hind.	Wheel Base. Rigid.	Engine.	Boiler Working Pressure.	Heating Surfaces. Tubes.	Firebox.	Total.	Grate Area.	Tractive Force at 75 % B.P.	Engine Weight. Adhesive.	Total.	Tank Capacity.	Fuel.
								Lbs.	Sq. Ft.	Sq. Ft.	Sq. Ft.	Sq. Ft.	Lbs.	Tons.	Tons.	Gals.	Cub. Ft.
L256	Arefecisse	15″ × 22″	2′ 4½″	3′ 7″	2′ 4½″	10′ 0″	24′ 0″	180	1031	100	1131	13·4	15,540	28·1	43·45	800	67·5
L295	Arelando	16″ × 20″	2′ 3″	3′ 3″	2′ 3″	7′ 6″	18′ 10″	150	920	72	992	16	14,769	31·9	42·75	880	67
4221E	Argempel	16″ × 20″	2′ 3″	3′ 3″	2′ 3″	9′ 8″	18′ 10″	160	845	98	943	13·5	15,754	29·5	39·3	850	51

Reference No. **L 295.**

Reference No. **4221 E.**

Tank Locomotives

Metre Gauge

Reference No. **E 1006.** **2.6.2. TYPE.**

Reference No. **3932 E.** **2.6.2. TYPE.**

Reference No.	Code Word.	Cylinders.	Wheels (Diam.).			Wheel Base.		Boiler Working Pressure.	Heating Surfaces.			Grate Area.	Tractive Force at 75 % B.P.	Engine Weight.		Tank Capacity.	Fuel.
		Diam. × Stroke.	Front.	Coupled.	Hind.	Rigid.	Engine.		Tubes.	Firebox.	Total.			Ad-hesive.	Total.		
								Lbs.	Sq. Ft.	Sq. Ft.	Sq. Ft.	Sq. Ft.	Lbs.	Tons.	Tons.	Gals.	Cub. Ft.
E1006	Arepennium	15¼″ × 18″	2′ 2″	3′ 4″	2′ 2″	9′ 5″	21′ 1″	160	652	66	718	12·5	12,554	25·6	36	900	56
3932E	Argematis	14½″ × 20″	2′ 3″	3′ 3″	2′ 3″	8′ 6″	21′ 3″	150	657	77	734	12·2	12,130	24·4	35·55	680	36
E1201	Arfaveis	14½″ × 18″	2′ 2″	3′ 0″	2′ 2″	9′ 6″	22′ 0″	160	629	65·5	694·5	12·2	12,615	22·9	32·1	600	45
4229E	Argennis	14½″ × 20″	2′ 3″	3′ 3″	2′ 3″	8′ 6″	21′ 3″	170	657	77	734	12·2	13,747	27·5	42	1100	60
L410	Arencaren	19″ × 20″	2′ 6″	3′ 6″	2′ 6″	12′ 0″	29′ 9″	200	1684	120	1804	27	25,785	52	83·1	2200	135

Reference No. **E 1201.** **2.6.2. TYPE.**

Reference No. **4229 E.** **2.6.2. TYPE.**

Reference No. **L 410.** **2.8.4. TYPE.**

Locomotives for the Smaller Gauges

Viz.: 3 ft. 0 in., 2 ft. 6 in., 2 ft. 0 in.

Locomotives with Tenders and Tank Locomotives 3 ft. 0 in. Gauge

Reference No. **L 445.** **4.8.0. TYPE.**

Reference No.	Code Word.	Cylinders.	Wheels (Diam.).			Wheel Base.			Boiler Working Pressure.	Heating Surfaces.			Grate Area.	Tractive Force at 75 % B.P.	Engine Weight.		Tender.		
		Diam. × Stroke.	Front.	Coupled.	Hind.	Rigid.	Engine.	E. and T.		Tubes.	Firebox.	Total.			Ad-hesive.	Total.	Tank Capacity.	Fuel.	Weight Full.
									Lbs.	Sq. Ft.	Sq. Ft.	Sq. Ft.	Sq. Ft.	Lbs.	Tons.	Tons.	Gals.	Cub. Ft.	Tons.
L445	Arendsuil	17″ × 20″	2′ 3″	3′ 3″	—	7′ 2″	19′ 9″	46′ 1″	180	1170	97	1267	23·6	20,000	38·2	47	2500	280	30·95
2571E	Argamasaba	16″ × 22″	2′ 6″	4′ 0″	—	9′ 0″	22′ 6″	43′ 7″	150	722	74	796	16	13,200	25 77	35·35	2000	300	30
3169E	Arganeau	15″ × 20″	2′ 6″	3′ 6″	2′ 6″	9′ 3″	18′ 0″	—	150	666	77	743	11·18	12,053	26·7	36·5	900	65	—
2890E	Argamassar	15″ × 20″	—	4′ 0″	4′ 0″	9′ 6″	15′ 0″	—	150	666	77	743	11·18	10,547	26·8	35·6	938	80	—

Reference No. **2571 E.** **4.6.0. TYPE.**

Reference No. **3169 E.** **2.6.2. TYPE.**

Reference No. **2890 E.** **0.6.2. TYPE.**

Tank Locomotives

3 ft. 0 in. Gauge

Reference No. **E 870.** **4.4.4. TYPE.**

Reference No.	Code Word.	Cylinders.	Wheels (Diam.).			Wheel Base.		Boiler Working Pressure.	Heating Surfaces.			Grate Area.	Tractive Force at 75 % B.P.	Engine Weight.		Tank Capacity.	Fuel.
		Diam. × Stroke.	Front.	Coupled.	Hind.	Rigid.	Engine.		Tubes.	Firebox.	Total.			Ad-hesive.	Total.		
								Lbs.	Sq. Ft.	Sq. Ft.	Sq. Ft.	Sq. Ft.	Lbs.	Tons.	Tons.	Gals.	Cub. Ft.
E870	Arenulous	14″ × 20″	2′ 3″	4′ 0″	2′ 3″	7′ 3″	26′ $1\frac{1}{2}$″	150	637	75	712	11·5	9,187	20·83	38·53	1000	120
E820	Arentiores	$14\frac{1}{2}$″ × 22″	3′ 0″	4′ 6″	3′ 0″	8′ 0″	21′ 0″	160	721	80	801	12	10,266	21·85	37·15	1000	114
E703	Arenicole	14″ × 20″	2′ 1″	3′ 6″	—	9′ 0″	16′ $7\frac{1}{2}$″	150	547	57	604	9·75	10,500	24·15	30·63	650	45

Reference No. **E 820.** **2.4.2. TYPE.**

Reference No. **E 703.** **4.6.0. TYPE.**

Locomotives with Tenders

2 ft. 6 in. Gauge

Reference No. **L 316.** **4.6.2. TYPE.**

Reference No.	Code Word.	Cylinders. Diam. × Stroke.	Wheels (Diam.). Front.	Wheels (Diam.). Coupled.	Wheels (Diam.). Hind.	Wheel Base. Rigid.	Wheel Base. Engine.	Wheel Base. E. and T.	Boiler Working Pressure.	Heating Surfaces. Tubes.	Heating Surfaces. Firebox.	Heating Surfaces. Total.	Grate Area.	Tractive Force at 75 % B.P.	Engine Weight. Ad-hesive.	Engine Weight. Total.	Tender. Tank Capacity.	Tender. Fuel.	Tender. Weight Full.
									Lbs.	Sq. Ft.	Sq. Ft.	Sq. Ft.	Sq. Ft.	Lbs.	Tons.	Tons.	Gals.	Cub. Ft.	Tons.
L316	Arelarja	14½″ × 18″	2′ 3″	3′ 6″	2′ 3″	8′ 0″	23′ 7½″	39′ 3″	160	898	66	964	17·5	10,812	20·6	33·6	1700	230	18·9
L144	Arduin	14½″ × 18″	2′ 3″	3′ 6″	2′ 3″	8′ 0″	23′ 7½″	39′ 3″	160	973	66	1039	17·5	10,812	20·4	33·25	1700	225	18 35
E981	Arepennis	11″ × 16″	2′ 0″	3′ 4″	—	5′ 9″	15′ 6″	27′ 9½″	140	366	36	402	6	5,082	—	14·6	800	45	9·4

Reference No. **L 144.** **4.6.2. TYPE.**

Reference No. **E 981.** **4.4.0. TYPE.**

Locomotives with Tenders

2 ft. 6 in. Gauge

Reference No. **E 788.** **0.4.2. TYPE.**

Reference No. **E 875.** **0.4.2. TYPE.**

Reference No. **L 434.** **2.8.0. TYPE.**

Reference No.	Code Word.	Cylinders.	Wheels (Diam.).			Wheel Base.			Boiler Working Pressure.	Heating Surfaces.			Grate Area.	Tractive Force at 75 % B.P.	Engine Weight.		Tender.		
		Diam. × Stroke.	Front.	Coupled.	Hind.	Rigid.	Engine.	E. and T.		Tubes.	Firebox.	Total.			Ad-hesive.	Total.	Tank Capacity.	Fuel.	Weight Full.
									Lbs.	Sq. Ft.	Sq. Ft.	Sq. Ft.	Sq. Ft.	Lbs.	Tons.	Tons.	Gals.	Cub. Ft.	Tons.
E788	Arenqueria	10″ × 18″	—	3′ 0″	2′ 0″	4′ 0″	10′ 0″	22′ 1¾″	140	383	39	422	7·6	5,250	10·7	13·3	650	45	7·55
E875	Areography	9″ × 14″	—	2′ 6″	2′ 1⅜″	4′ 6″	11′ 6″	24′ 5″	175	333	47	380	11·3	4,960	11·38	14·5	750	200	11·8
L434	Arendsoog	16½″ × 20″	2′ 3″	3′ 1½″	—	10′ 7″	17′ 1″	44′ 4″	180	1148	88	1236	20·1	19,602	42·3	46·3	2,500	280	30·75
L385	Arenasses	14½″ × 18″	1′ 11″	2′ 10″	2′ 3″	9′ 7″	22′ 10″	38′ 5½″	170	1112	79	1191	20·5	14,191	28	39·1	1,700	230	18·9

Reference No. **L 385.** **2.8.2. TYPE.**

Tank Locomotives

2 ft. 6 in. Gauge

Reference No. **L 430.** **0.4.0. TYPE.**

Reference No. **E 1187.** **0.4.2. TYPE.**

Reference No.	Code Word.	Cylinders.	Wheels (Diam.).		Wheel Base.		Boiler Working Pressure.	Heating Surfaces.			Grate Area.	Tractive Force at 75 % B.P.	Engine Weight.		Tank Capacity.	Fuel.
		Diam. × Stroke.	Coupled.	Hind.	Rigid.	Engine.		Tubes.	Firebox.	Total.			Ad-hesive.	Total.		
							Lbs.	Sq. Ft.	Sq. Ft.	Sq. Ft.	Sq. Ft.	Lbs.	Tons.	Tons.	Gals.	Cub. Ft.
L430	Arendsei	12″ × 16″	2′ 6″	—	5′ 6″	5′ 6″	140	390	36	426	7	8,064	17	17	400	20
E1187	Arevessava	12″ × 16″	2′ 6″	1′ 9″	5′ 6″	10′ 9″	140	400	50	450	13·2	8,064	16·95	21·55	500	60
E1186	Arevessais	11½″ × 14″	2′ 2″	1′ 6″	5′ 3″	11′ 3″	150	391	39	430	9·25	8,011	15·35	19	500	60
E1197	Arfasato	8″ × 14″	2′ 6″	1′ 9″	4′ 3″	9′ 4″	160	187	28	215	7	3,584	10	12·5	200	33

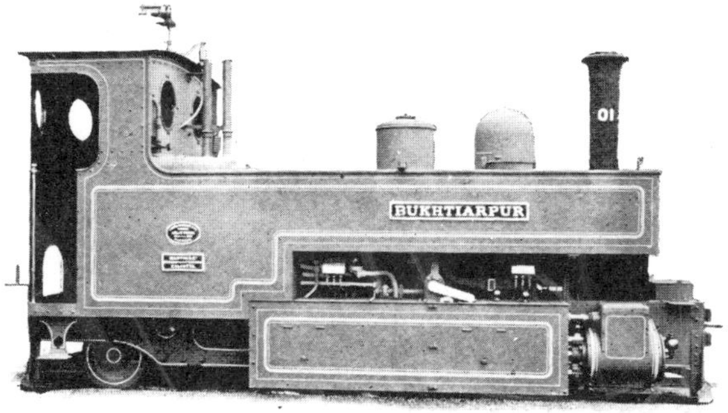

Reference No. **E 1197.** **0.4.2. TYPE.**

Reference No. **E 1186.** **0.4.2. TYPE.**

Tank Locomotives

2 ft. 6 in. Gaug

Reference No. **L 331.** **4.6.4. TYPE.**

Reference No.	Code Word.	Cylinders.	Wheels (Diam.).			Wheel Base.		Boiler Working Pressure.	Heating Surfaces.			Grate Area.	Tractive Force at 75 % B.P.	Engine Weight.		Tank Capacity.	Fuel.
		Diam. × Stroke.	Front.	Coupled.	Hind.	Rigid.	Engine.		Tubes.	Firebox.	Total.			Ad-hesive.	Total.		
								Lbs.	Sq. Ft.	Sq. Ft.	Sq. Ft.	Sq. Ft.	Lbs.	Tons.	Tons.	Gals.	Cub. Ft.
L331	Arelaseis	14″ × 20″	2′ 0″	3′ 0″	2′ 0″	6′ 8″	23′ 8″	160	731	66	797	19	13,066	25·35	46·1	1200	146
L120	Arduamente	12″ × 16″	—	3′ 0½″	2′ 0½″	6′ 11″	17′ 2″	160	500	54	554	11·9	7,574	16·15	26·3	400	90
L332	Arelasemos	14″ × 16″	1′ 9″	2′ 6″	1′ 9″	6′ 0″	17′ 6″	180	695	57	752	14	14,112	25·42	34·97	650	75

Reference No. **L 120.** **0.6.4. TYPE.**

Reference No. **L 332.** **2.6.2. TYPE.**

I

8.4. Type

Tank Locomotives

2 ft. 6 in. Gauge

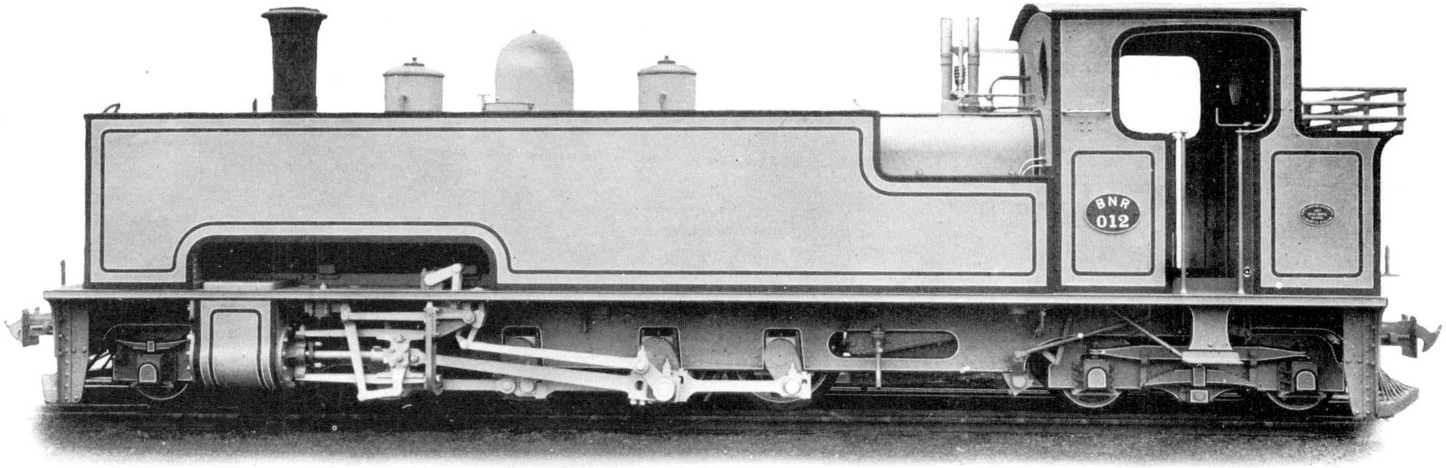

Reference No. **L 135.**

Reference No.	Code Word.	CYLINDERS.	WHEELS (Diam.).			WHEEL BASE.		Boiler Working Pressure.	HEATING SURFACES.			Grate Area.	Tractive Force at 75 % B.P.	ENGINE WEIGHT.		Tank Capacity.	Fuel.
		Diam. × Stroke.	Front.	Coupled.	Hind.	Rigid.	Engine.		Tubes.	Firebox.	Total.			Ad-hesive.	Total.		
								Lbs.	Sq. Ft.	Sq. Ft.	Sq. Ft.	Sq. Ft.	Lbs.	Tons.	Tons.	Gals.	Cub. Ft.
L135	ARDUIDAD	14½″ × 18″	1′ 11″	2′ 10″	1′ 11″	9′ 7″	27′ 6″	160	837	67	904	16·5	13,357	26·8	42·35	1400	90
E1188	AREVESSOU	14½″ × 18″	1′ 11″	2′ 10″	1′ 11″	9′ 7″	27′ 6″	160	837	67	904	16·5	13,357	24·4	38·85	800	90
L58	ARDESCIMUS	14″ × 18″	1′ 11″	2′ 10″	1′ 11″	9′ 7″	26′ 9″	150	693	62	755	15·3	11,673	22·5	34·2	600	45

Reference No. **E 1188.**

Reference No. **L 58.**

Locomotives with Tenders and Tank Locomotives 2 ft. 0 in. Gauge

Reference No. **L 319.** **0.6.0. TYPE.**

Reference No.	Code Word.	Cylinders.	Wheels (Diam.).		Wheel Base.			Boiler Working Pressure.	Heating Surfaces.			Grate Area.	Tractive Force at 75 % B.P.	Engine Weight.		Tender.		
		Diam. × Stroke.	Coupled.	Hind.	Rigid.	Engine.	E. and T.		Tubes.	Firebox.	Total.			Ad-hesive.	Total.	Tank Capacity.	Fuel.	Weight Full.
								Lbs.	Sq. Ft.	Sq. Ft.	Sq. Ft.	Sq. Ft.	Lbs.	Tons.	Tons.	Gals.	Cub. Ft.	Tons.
L319	Arelaron	12″ × 16″	2′ 6″	—	6′ 0″	6′ 0″	23′ 10″	160	491	54	545	14	9,216	20·3	20·3	800	100	10·05
E1185	Areumatico	8″ × 14″	2′ 6″	1′ 9″	4′ 6″	10′ 3″	—	150	192	29	221	7·7	3,360	10·75	13·5	250	45	—
E1081	Arestins	7″ × 12″	2′ 6″	1′ 9″	4′ 9″	9′ 9″	—	150	192	26	218	6·5	2,220	10·2	12·5	250	45	—

Reference No. **E 1185.** **0.4.2. TYPE.**

Reference No. **E 1081.** **0.4.2. TYPE.**

Tank Locomotives

2 ft. 0 in. Gauge

Reference No. **E 1195.** **0.4.0. TYPE.**

Reference No. **E 1023.** **0.4.0. TYPE.**

Reference No.	Code Word.	Cylinders. Diam. × Stroke.	Wheels (Diam.). Front.	Wheels (Diam.). Coupled.	Wheels (Diam.). Hind.	Wheel Base. Rigid.	Wheel Base. Engine.	Boiler Working Pressure.	Heating Surfaces. Tubes.	Heating Surfaces. Firebox.	Heating Surfaces. Total.	Grate Area.	Tractive Force at 75 % B.P.	Engine Weight. Adhesive.	Engine Weight. Total.	Tank Capacity.	Fuel.
								Lbs.	Sq. Ft.	Sq. Ft.	Sq. Ft.	Sq. Ft.	Lbs.	Tons.	Tons.	Gals.	Cub. Ft.
E1195	Arfarem	6″ × 9″	—	1′ 8″	—	2′ 7″	2′ 7″	140	91	13	104	1·7	1,701	4·8	4·8	90	11
E1023	Arepita	6″ × 9″	—	1′ 8″	—	2′ 7″	2′ 7″	140	70	13	83	1·87	1,701	3·02	3·02	22	—
E941	Areostilo	11″ × 14″	—	2′ 2″	—	5′ 6″	5′ 6″	140	276	40	316	9	6,841	13·35	13·35	400	33
E932	Areometro	9″ × 14″	1′ 9″	2′ 6″	1′ 9″	4′ 3″	14′ 8″	140	210	28	238	5·17	3,969	8	15·9	250	30
E1088	Aretaics	12″ × 16″	—	2′ 6″	1′ 9″	5′ 6″	10′ 3″	140	341	34	375	9·5	8,064	16·65	19·65	550	67

eference No. **E 932.** **2.4.2. TYPE.**

Reference No. **E 941.** **0.4.0. TYPE.**

Reference No. **E 1088.** **0.4.2. TYPE.**

"ABT" Combined Rack and Adhesion Locomotive for the Metre Gaug

Reference No. L 371. **0.8.2. TYPE.**

Locomotives of this type are constructed to work on Mountain Railways, which have, on their steeper grades, a **Rack-Rail** laid in the centre between the two ordinary rails. They are fitted with a pair of Outside Cylinder Engines for working in the usual way by the **Adhesion** of the wheels. They are also fitted with a pair of Inside Cylinder Engines for working, through a pinion, on to the **Rack-Rail,** and acting quite independently of the Adhesion Engines.

THE LOADS STATED ARE EXCLUSIVE OF THE WEIGHT OF THE ENGINE.

Reference No.	Code Word.	Type.	Gauge.	Load in Tons.				
				On Combined Rack and Adhesion Sections.				Adhesion only.
				On 1 in $12\frac{1}{2}$.	On 1 in 16.	On 1 in 20.	On 1 in 25.	On 1 in 25.
L371	Arenamento	0.8.2.	3′ $3\frac{3}{8}$″	65	90	115	140	130

"ABT" Combination Rack and Adhesion Locomotives

Reference No. **L 67.** **0.6.2. TYPE.** **Metre Gauge**

Locomotives of this type are constructed to work on Mountain Railways, which have, on their steeper grades, a **Rack-Rail** laid in the centre between the two ordinary rails. They are fitted with a pair of Outside Cylinder Engines for working in the usual way by the **Adhesion** of the wheels. They are also fitted with a pair of Inside Cylinder Engines for working, through a pinion, on to the **Rack-Rail**, and acting quite independently of the Adhesion Engines.

THE LOADS STATED ARE EXCLUSIVE OF THE WEIGHT OF THE ENGINE.

Reference No.	Code Word.	Type.	Gauge.	Load in Tons.				
				On Combined Rack and Adhesion Sections.				Adhesion only.
				On 1 in 12½.	On 1 in 16.	On 1 in 20.	On 1 in 25.	On 1 in 25.
4085E	ARGEMONIAM	0.4.2.	3′ 6″	45	60	75	90	55
L152	ARDUITADE	0.6.0.	3′ 6″	60	75	95	120	90
L67	ARDESCUNT	0.6.2.	3′ 3⅜″	65	85	110	135	100

Reference No. **L 152.** **0.6.0. TYPE.** **3 ft. 6 in. Gauge.**

Reference No. **4085 E.** **0.4.2. TYPE.** **3 ft. 6 in. Gauge.**